"Terence is deeply interested in matters affecting the lives of Singaporeans and he makes a huge contribution by providing insightful perspectives and analysis of the issues of the day. His willingness to articulate his thoughts with clarity engenders broader awareness and provides input for policy-making considerations. His collection of published essays is a must-read for anyone who wants to understand the challenges that the nation and Singaporeans are dealing with."

Adam Abdur Rahman, Head of Corporate Affairs, Citi Singapore and ASEAN

"Terence Ho's *Governing Well* is a *tour de force* that outlines Singapore's approach to public policy: an unrelenting commitment to innovation and continuous improvement; a search for balance that blends economic performance and social progress; and a focus on problem solving in the short term that leads to better outcomes in the longer term.

Each chapter of this book invites the reader to explore a different area of public policy, putting the key issues into perspective. The author skilfully reminds readers of what was accomplished before to gain a deeper appreciation of the significance of recent government initiatives. In doing so, he raises probing questions and provides insightful suggestions, encouraging new thinking to reframe issues from an evolving perspective.

The most important contribution of this book is what it reveals in aggregate. In many ways, this book describes an approach to governance that is able to evolve and adapt to changing needs and circumstances. It is a hopeful statement about governing in the fast-changing world we live in."

Jocelyne Bourgon, Founding President, Public Governance International; formerly Clerk of the Privy Council and Secretary to the Cabinet, Canada (Canada's most senior public servant), and Chairperson of the United Nations Committee of Experts in Public Administration

"In this collection of his essays first published in the major news media in Singapore, Terence provides insightful perspectives of what it takes to govern a city and country well amid changes and challenges. By analysing the multifaceted nature of Singapore policymaking in terms of its economic, social, and political dimensions, these essays collectively reiterate the sensitivity of contextual factors and remind us of the importance of a principled, adaptive leadership and a proactive, involved citizenry. I highly recommend this book to anyone interested in governing well, especially in Singapore but also beyond."

David Chan, Lee Kong Chian Professor of Psychology, and Director, Behavioural Sciences Initiative, Singapore Management University

"Serving in the social and healthcare sectors, I got to know and work with Terence when he was General Manager of the South East Community Development Council, before his posting to the Ministry of Finance. Being a former senior civil servant intimately involved in policymaking and implementing policies on the ground, Terence is able to provide great insights on policies and how these policies affect the community.

Governing Well is a collection of thoughts on Singapore's governance and what it takes for the country to succeed. Policies are explained simply with interesting perspectives and insights, covering not just the 'what' but the 'why'. At the same time, the book provides thought-provoking ideas and suggestions for our complex and turbulent times."

Albert Ching, CEO, Singapore Cancer Society, and former President, YMCA of Singapore

"Terence's commentaries from 2021 to 2022 allow readers to easily assimilate ideas on important societal matters in Singapore's context. These are matters close to the heart of the person on the street. I have personally found the articles illuminative of various government policies. As an entrepreneur, I appreciate the clear and concise presentation of ideas and information. I strongly recommend this book to the business community for its contribution in explaining the rationale for Singapore's socio-economic policies, while contributing thought leadership in the formulation of business policies. I congratulate Terence on his book and I look forward to reading more of his expositions in the future."

Douglas Foo, Chairman, Sakae Holdings; formerly President of the Singapore Manufacturing Federation, Vice-Chairman of the Singapore Business Federation and Nominated Member of Parliament

"Terence writes about all the important issues facing Singapore in the new and complex world where continued success requires fresh thinking and new approaches. He may not have all the answers but he is always balanced and thoughtful."

Han Fook Kwang, Editor-at-Large, *The Straits Times*, and Senior Fellow, S. Rajaratnam School of International Studies, Nanyang Technological University

"While pursuing a career in the civil service, Terence Ho has also taken the road less travelled through a detour into academia at the Lee Kuan Yew School of Public Policy. This book of his essays bears testimony that this has been time well spent."

Peter Ho, Chairman, Urban Redevelopment Authority of Singapore, and former Head of the Singapore Civil Service

"Terence Ho is one of the rare breed of academics who has had intimate, first-hand knowledge of the intricacies of policymaking. And it shows — his commentaries are lucid, well-informed, and thoughtful. Above all, his ideas and suggestions do not come from an ivory tower. What he has to say provides very real food for thought — for researchers, policymakers and the interested layman alike — when it comes to the tough choices that will have to be made in an increasingly challenging environment."

Shashi Jayakumar, Senior Fellow and Head, Centre of Excellence for National Security, S. Rajaratnam School of International Studies, Nanyang Technological University

"Terence Ho is a voice of reason among Singapore's thought leaders. Having served in the Civil Service before joining academia, he is able to straddle the two worlds. I am happy to recommend this book."

Tommy Koh, Ambassador-at-Large, Singapore Ministry of Foreign Affairs, and Emeritus Professor of Law, National University of Singapore

"With his many years as a policy practitioner in the Ministry of Finance, Terence's commentaries train his economist lens on the full range of public policy issues spanning leadership, R&D, labour policies and fiscal management.

Government expenditure is the largest single fiscal lever that can be exercised, to great impact. Hence, it is imperative to get good returns by framing the desired outcomes well. To this end, the critiques and observations in this book have deconstructed government policies to help the broader public understand the economic and social objectives as well as the many inherent trade-offs, while also revealing nuances not fully appreciated at first glance.

The topics in this timely collection reflect the dynamics of a rapidly changing world, where social upheaval, economic restructuring and disruption in work modes have become the norm. The book also helps to illumine the multifarious impact which the COVID-19 pandemic has had on society."

Lien Choong Luen, General Manager, Gojek Singapore, and President, Singapore Athletics

"It is refreshing and inspiring to read observations and commentaries on events as they happen. Terence Ho brings us to watch the drama with keenness and understanding as he takes us through a whole slew of changes in public policy impinging on all aspects of life in Singapore, social and economic, personal and collective. Don't miss out!"

Lim Siong Guan, Professor of Practice, Lee Kuan Yew School of Public Policy, National University of Singapore; formerly Head of the Singapore Civil Service, Chairman of the Singapore Economic Development Board, and Group President of the Government of Singapore Investment Corporation (GIC)

"Terence's perspectives over a wide range of issues are clear and balanced. He has been able to make even some of the more complicated issues easy to understand."

Lim Soo Hoon, former Permanent Secretary (Community Development, Public Service Division and Finance Performance) — Singapore's first female Permanent Secretary

"Terence Ho provides keen insights on a range of social and economic issues facing Singapore. These highly readable articles not only explain the rationale behind many public policies and how they have served Singapore well but also the need for fresh thinking and policy innovation if Singapore is to continue doing well amid a changing environment."

Ravi Menon, Managing Director, Monetary Authority of Singapore

"Terence Ho, a former colleague in the Ministry of Finance, is a highly inquisitive and analytical person who would often offer thought-provoking perspectives that prompted me and others to ponder more deeply about issues that matter to our society and citizens. I highly recommend his book."

Ngien Hoon Ping, Group CEO, SMRT Corporation

"The emerging future is one of increasing contestation and ambiguities in Singapore, necessitating more consultation and participation. People must be co-creators, not merely 'consumers', of good governance — we must have a stake in this country we call home. Terence's pointed perspectives across diverse issues are an important read and a valuable resource for this new social compact towards a more inclusive and equal society."

Anthea Ong, social entrepreneur and former Nominated Member of Parliament

"For more than a decade I have enjoyed the opportunity to work with the Singapore Civil Service College. I've learned much about the nation's 'exceptionalism' during this period. But Terence Ho's series of succinct yet incisive articles has provided me, an admirer of Singapore's progress, with a window into the ever-widening range of economic and social issues that are emerging. His thoughtful prognosis gives me confidence that Singapore can continue to rise to the challenges ahead, creating its own brand of 'constructive, competitive democracy'. Taken together, Ho's pieces have persuaded me that Singapore can remain a beacon of hope for others."

Peter Shergold, Chancellor, Western Sydney University, and former Secretary of the Department of the Prime Minister and Cabinet, Australia (Australia's most senior public servant)

"This book is a fascinating, insightful and highly readable compilation on Singapore, the socio-economic, fiscal and political developments in recent years. Drawing on his strong experience in government service and deep personal insights into public policymaking, Terence has helped us to understand better Singapore's approaches towards social and economic development and the model of governance that is uniquely Singapore's moving forward."

Tan Kwang Cheak, CEO, Agency for Integrated Care

"Terence Ho's book could not have come at a more opportune time. The uncertainties and complexities that lie ahead behove us to look at what has been done before, avoid past mistakes but more importantly chart new paths to help us sail into the unknown with enough confidence to deal with these challenges. Professor Ho's unique perspective of once being an 'insider' and now looking at policies from the viewpoint of an academic, will certainly help to bring diversity in thinking on policy formulation. I am confident that this book will help those in the public sector to see the impact of policies from many different perspectives."

Yaacob Ibrahim, Professor of Engineering and Advisor to the President, Singapore Institute of Technology; former Minister in charge of Community Development, Youth and Sports, the Environment and Water Resources, Communications and Information, Cyber Security and Muslim Affairs in the Singapore Cabinet

Governing Well

Reflections on Singapore and Beyond

Other World Scientific Title by the Author

Refreshing the Singapore System:
Recalibrating Socio-Economic Policy for the 21st Century
ISBN: 978-981-123-653-2
ISBN: 978-981-125-355-3 (pbk)

Governing Well

Reflections on Singapore and Beyond

W. L. Terence Ho

Lee Kuan Yew School of Public Policy,
National University of Singapore, Singapore

World Scientific

JERSEY · LONDON · SINGAPORE · BEIJING · SHANGHAI · HONG KONG · TAIPEI · CHENNAI · TOKYO

Published by

World Scientific Publishing Co. Pte. Ltd.
5 Toh Tuck Link, Singapore 596224
USA office: 27 Warren Street, Suite 401-402, Hackensack, NJ 07601
UK office: 57 Shelton Street, Covent Garden, London WC2H 9HE

National Library Board, Singapore Cataloguing in Publication Data
Name(s): Ho, W. L. Terence, author.
Title: Governing well : reflections on Singapore and beyond / W. L. Terence Ho.
Description: Singapore : World Scientific Publishing Co. Pte. Ltd., [2023]
Identifier(s): ISBN 978-981-12-6631-7 (hardback) | 978-981-12-6632-4 (ebook for institutions) |
    978-981-12-6633-1 (ebook for individuals)
Subject(s): LCSH: Singapore--Politics and government. | Singapore--Economic policy. |
    Singapore--Social policy.
Classification: DDC 320.95957--dc23

British Library Cataloguing-in-Publication Data
A catalogue record for this book is available from the British Library.

For any available supplementary material, please visit
https://www.worldscientific.com/worldscibooks/10.1142/13142#t=suppl

Desk Editor: Jiang Yulin

Typeset by Stallion Press
Email: enquiries@stallionpress.com

Preface

It wasn't planned.

I did not set out to be a writer of newspaper columns (although that had indeed been a childhood aspiration). In mid-2021, I approached Singapore's flagship English daily, *The Straits Times*, for a review of my book, *Refreshing the Singapore System: Recalibrating Socio-Economic Policy for the 21st Century*. The reply was, to paraphrase: we no longer do book reviews, but you're welcome to contribute an op-ed bearing your name, position and title of your book.

And so I wrote my first piece on the evolution of Singapore's social policies, a major theme of my book. A few days after this was published, the Government made a significant policy announcement. As this touched on an area of work I was familiar with (from an earlier stint at the Ministry of Finance), I felt compelled to pen a commentary in response.

Subsequently, I was invited by *The Straits Times* to be a regular contributor with the broad mandate to write on any issue of the day.

In early 2022, I reconnected with a former colleague who had become a news editor at Mediacorp's Asian news network CNA. She invited me to contribute an opinion piece on the impending Goods and Services Tax hike. This launched my relationship with CNA, for which I have now contributed several commentaries. Invitations to write for TODAY, as well as overseas publications, followed.

Why do I write? It is to organise and give expression to the many thoughts percolating in my mind on how Singapore can find its way forward in a changing world with heightened geopolitical risks and domestic stresses. Singapore may have acquired a reputation for good governance, but the challenges facing the city-state are growing and evolving. This requires fresh thinking — not only on the part of public officers, but also by citizens, businesses, non-governmental organisations and other stakeholders.

Topics such as economic development, education and social support are relevant not only to Singapore, but also to many other countries grappling with similar challenges and constraints. However, each country has a different context. Public policy is never made in a vacuum; socio-political factors are always at play.

Singapore, while recognised for its economic and social achievements, has attracted criticism from foreign observers for its ostensibly draconian laws and curtailment of dissent. The past two decades have however seen Singapore take significant strides in the direction of greater political openness and ideological contestation. Many wonder: will Singapore drift inexorably towards a Western-style liberal democracy, or will it remain moored to its authoritarian legacy?

I for one would like to see Singapore develop its own brand of constructive, competitive democracy that harnesses the competition of ideas to build up rather than divide society. If Singapore is able to achieve this, it can, in a modest way, be a city on a hill — a home where its citizens can fulfil their aspirations, and a beacon of hope for others.

This collection of essays could not have been put together without the support of *The Straits Times*, *CNA* and *TODAY*. I appreciate the opportunities I have been given to contribute opinion pieces and for permission to reproduce them in this book.

My writing has benefitted much from the editorial input of Chua Mui Hoong, Audrey Quek, Grace Ho, Lin Suling, Charlene Tan and Kor Kian Beng. I am thankful for their support and guidance.

Credit also goes to my World Scientific editor, Jiang Yulin, for patiently shepherding *Governing Well* through to publication.

Over the years, my views on public policy have been shaped by colleagues and mentors from the Singapore Public Service. As a writer, I have received much encouragement from family and friends, as well as readers who have reached out to me with their views and feedback. To all of them I owe a debt of gratitude.

Most of all, I would like to thank my wife Grace who has provided wise counsel and incisive comments on my writing. Her unstinting support has made all the difference.

Contents

Preface   xi

Part A   Social and Employment Policy   **1**

Singapore's Social Policies: New Normal or Still an
    Exceptional System?   3

Progressive Wage Model 2.0: A Step Closer to a More
    Inclusive Society   9

Foreign Manpower: Making the Global Talent Approach
    Work for Singapore   15

Investing in Education: Returns, Risks and Career Resilience   21

As Singapore's Demographics Change, So Too Must Mindsets   27

What It Means to Live Well in Singapore   33

Ride-Hailing and Delivery Jobs Are Here to Stay — Let's
    Make Them Work   39

Improved Meritocracy Can Focus on Skills, Training and
    Career Progression   45

Part B   Economic Development and Public Finance   **49**

Growing Global Champions with Roots in Singapore   51

Getting More Bang from the R&D Buck   57

Why the Need to Raise the GST Now?   63

Let's Bite the Bullet on Taxes and Manpower Rules   69

Greater Social Spending and Redistribution Rest on Economic
    Growth and Government Prudence   75

Budget 2022 Sets the Pace for Singapore's Transformation   81

Many Lines of Defence Are Needed to Keep Inflation at Bay   87

Call the Sports Hub Public-Private Partnership a Failure or Not,
    That is Not the Point   93

Addressing Inflation While Staying the Course on
    Medium-Term Priorities   97

Part C   Politics and Society   101

Making Democracy Work   103

A Year of Obstinate Hope   109

In a Storm-Tossed World, Who's Going to Steer Your Ship?   115

Realism, Rules and Empathy All Matter in a Turbulent World   121

Strengthening the Middle Ground   125

Seizing the Opportunity to Move Singapore Forward   129

Renewing an Exceptional Singapore   133

Home, Truly   139

Part A
Social and Employment Policy

Singapore's Social Policies: New Normal or Still an Exceptional System?

First published in The Straits Times on 19 August 2021

Public policy announcements are always in the news — a new scheme here, an enhancement there. Few, however, pause to reflect on what these add up to. Occasionally, the Government may string together a narrative for a major speech such as during the Budget debate or Committee of Supply, but the message is often lost among the policy details.

As a director at the Ministry of Finance from 2010 to 2016, I felt that there was a story worth telling about how Singapore has quietly but systematically overhauled its socio-economic system since the turn of the century.

We started off with a system that was a significant outlier in terms of social protection. In 2004, National University of Singapore professor M. Ramesh described Singapore as "a special case in the region because of its tenacity in resisting the expansion of state provision of income protection, and because of the extent to which it has gone to encourage and/ or compel individuals to meet contingencies on their own".

American political scientist Ron Haskins, following a visit here in 2011, put a more positive spin on this, extolling Singapore as a "crucible of individual responsibility" that has created "one of the best educated, most disciplined and most self-reliant populations in the world".

The Singapore system is founded on self-reliance or individual responsibility towards self, family and community, also described as "reward for work, and work for reward". Through their Central Provident Fund (CPF) savings, Singaporeans provide for their own housing, healthcare and retirement needs, supplemented by government subsidies.

To encourage work and enterprise, taxes are kept low and fiscal redistribution limited. The unemployed are required to tap personal savings, along with family and community help, before turning to the state for financial support as a last recourse. At the same time, the state invests heavily in education and skills for a competitive workforce and self-reliant citizenry.

The Singapore system worked remarkably well, as decades of strong economic growth lifted incomes and improved the lives of most Singaporeans. Rising living standards in turn buttressed public support for policies that promoted long-term economic growth.

RISING COSTS AND INEQUALITY

The system was, however, bound to run up against the same challenges confronting other advanced economies, notably slowing economic growth, rising costs and growing inequality.

Global competition and technological advances have upended traditional business models, putting jobs at risk even as Singaporeans' career and income aspirations have risen. Singapore is also among the world's most rapidly ageing societies, with healthcare costs rising steeply and workforce growth tapering off after years of expansion.

While globalisation has brought outsized benefits to those with skills in demand, it has also pegged back wages in jobs where the supply of skills is abundant, whether due to the influx of foreign workers into Singapore or competition from abroad in exportable sectors.

The concentration of talent and wealth in Singapore confers on the nation a location premium, enabling higher incomes than Singaporeans would otherwise command based on their skills. However, this has also widened inequality and driven up the cost of living. Maintaining social mobility will become ever more difficult as Singapore society stratifies, with the affluent passing on accumulated wealth and economic advantages to their offspring.

Entering the 21st century, these challenges have necessitated a rebalancing between self-reliance or personal effort, and public or collective support.

Structural transfers to the less well-off, notably the Workfare Income Supplement, the Silver Support Scheme, and the Goods and Services Tax (GST) Voucher, have been introduced and enhanced. Social risk pooling, through the introduction of CPF LIFE, MediShield Life and CareShield Life, has taken on a critical role in healthcare and retirement provision, alongside mandatory savings. Housing and healthcare subsidies have been stepped up, particularly through the Enhanced CPF Housing Grant and the Pioneer and Merdeka Generation packages.

Cumulatively, these moves have taken Singapore a long way since the early 2000s. Singapore now has a more comprehensive social security system, with many of the social programmes found in other advanced economies.

While the absence of a minimum wage and unemployment insurance still stands out, changes are on the way. The Government has indicated that the Progressive Wage Model, a system of sectoral minimum wages with prescribed wage ladders and upgrading pathways, will be extended to more sectors and eventually the whole economy. The National Trades Union Congress, meanwhile, is exploring the design of an unemployment insurance scheme.

END OF EXCEPTIONALISM?

Does this, then, signal the end of Singapore exceptionalism in social policy? Certainly, a case can be made that Singapore has bowed to the same pressures faced by many other advanced economies and maturing societies. In designing social policy changes, however, the Government has hewed to its principle of upholding individual responsibility and personal effort.

For instance, Workfare rewards work; social insurance premiums are often paid for by one's own CPF savings. In lieu of a statutory minimum wage, the Government is expanding the coverage of progressive wages which are tied to productivity and skills upgrading, and hence more in keeping with the spirit of "work for reward".

Upstream intervention continues to be prioritised — public investment in education and skills has been enhanced, brought forward to early childhood, and extended through life. Tax incentives encourage community giving, while welfare benefits remain residual rather than universal. Social support is provided in a way that is consistent with the Government's socio-economic principles, but the principles themselves are being interpreted more broadly to accommodate new forms of support.

Singapore also retains unique strengths compared with other systems, including high savings and home ownership rates, and investment returns on state reserves which have become the largest source of government revenue, ahead of even corporate income tax.

Notwithstanding the suite of policies already introduced to shore up social protection, the question is what more is needed to sustain the social compact in the face of economic volatility and the relentless upward pressure on inequality. With COVID-19 and climate change adding to the structural and demographic driving forces reshaping Singapore's economy and society, it is timely to reflect on this.

The Government can continue to increase the coverage and support rates of schemes such as Workfare and Silver Support. To strengthen support for displaced workers, employment facilitation could be complemented by unemployment insurance or a precautionary savings scheme (perhaps riding on CPF), supplemented by government top-ups for the less well-off. It is also important to get more self-employed persons into the CPF system so that they can accumulate savings for their medical needs and retirement.

While shifting to the highly redistributive Nordic model of universal social welfare may be a step too far for Singapore, one possibility is for the Government to provide a "social dividend" from the state's investment income. This could be framed as supporting national solidarity rather than as a form of residual support for the less well-off.

Unlike Workfare, Silver Support or the GST Voucher, the dividend would be given to all Singaporeans but may have to be tiered according to wealth or cumulative income in order to keep the fiscal cost manageable. If tied to some measure of economic performance, it could engender support for policies that promote growth and keep the economy open, while helping to offset the cost of living in a global city.

Together with other forms of social support with which it could potentially be rationalised, a regular social dividend (in contrast to ad hoc sharing of Budget surpluses) could give Singaporeans greater peace of mind to ride out the vicissitudes of economic cycles, especially for those whose jobs and incomes have been threatened by economic restructuring or the impact of COVID-19.

To sustain social mobility and keep inequality at bay, upstream investment in education and skills remains a priority. Concurrent downstream efforts, such as imposing more progressive taxes on incomes and particularly wealth, may also be necessary to preserve fairness and social cohesion, so that inherited advantage does not undercut the principle of "work for reward".

Further reducing reliance on lower-skilled foreign workers is a must to drive productivity and raise local wages across the economy, while recognising that Singapore cannot divest the bulk of the foreign workforce without shrinking the breadth of its economic activity. As for higher-skilled foreigners, the balance must be found between assuring Singaporeans of fair opportunities for jobs and career development, and keeping Singapore open to reap the considerable advantages that come with being a global city.

Finally, public agencies must be zealous in managing expenditure — not tightfisted when money ought to be spent, but constantly checking the tendency towards excess. In the provision of public services and amenities, it is important to offer lower-cost options to Singaporeans. There must also be strong effort to develop and sustain common spaces, which are crucial in forging a shared national identity.

The Singapore system would require, as Senior Minister Tharman Shanmugaratnam has suggested, the "social empathy and solidarity" advanced by the left, together with the "ethic of personal responsibility and effort" espoused by the right — personal effort with collective support, in short. This may be the ticket to Singapore's continued exceptionalism in the new normal.

Progressive Wage Model 2.0: A Step Closer to a More Inclusive Society

First published in The Straits Times on 19 August 2021

At the National Day Rally last Sunday, Prime Minister Lee Hsien Loong announced that the Government would accept the recommendations of the Tripartite Workgroup on Lower-Wage Workers. The centrepiece is the expansion of the Progressive Wage Model (PWM) to cover over eight in 10 lower-wage local workers.

What will this mean for lower-wage workers, businesses and society at large? Here are three key takeaways: First, PWM 2.0 — as I call the expanded initiative — will largely achieve what a minimum wage is intended to do. Second, it will be challenging to implement PWM as it was originally envisaged. Third, its success will require broad stakeholder consensus on transforming Singapore into a more inclusive society.

PWM 1.0: ADDRESSING "CHEAP SOURCING"

The PWM, introduced in 2012, has emerged as a key prong in the national strategy to raise wages. It had a much narrower aim at the outset — to tackle the problem of "cheap sourcing" in the cleaning sector.

Cleaning companies would submit low bids to win contracts and then rehire existing cleaners at lower wages. This kept cleaners' wages stagnant for many years in the 2000s. Initially voluntary, PWM became mandatory for all cleaning contracts from September 2015. The scheme was later widened to include the security and landscaping sectors, which were similarly prone to "cheap sourcing", and more recently the lift and escalator maintenance sector.

While the PWM can be considered a sectoral minimum wage, it does not just set a wage floor but also a wage ladder corresponding to different levels of skill and responsibility. The link to skills reflects the Government's intent to have wages rise in line with, and not ahead of, productivity.

The real median wages of local workers in the PWM sectors rose on average by a cumulative 31 per cent between 2014 and 2019, compared with a 21 per cent increase at the median for all sectors. This was to a large extent catch-up wage growth for these workers after years of stagnating pay.

However, PWM 1.0 covered only about a tenth of the approximately 283,000 workers in the bottom 20 per cent of the wage distribution. The limited scope of the PWM and pace of implementation prompted calls for Singapore to enact a statutory minimum wage. Proponents argue that this would provide an immediate wage floor for all workers, complementing the PWM.

PWM 2.0: A MINIMUM WAGE BY ANY OTHER NAME

The Government's approach to help lower-wage workers has been to build on Workfare and PWM instead. It was announced in March this year that PWM would be extended to cover up to 218,000 workers including those from the waste management, retail and food services sectors. Among the remaining low-wage workers left uncovered: a sizeable number who work as clerks and drivers in many different sectors.

The challenge has been to find a suitable regulatory lever to implement PWM in these sectors and occupations, especially where there are no existing licensing requirements and the Government is not a major service buyer.

The lever which the Tripartite Workgroup settled on is a familiar one: foreign worker access. As many firms — micro enterprises excepted — hire foreign workers, this provides the Government with the means of implementing PWM widely. For sectors and occupations that have yet to develop tripartite-backed wage ladders, imposing a wage floor — the "Local Qualifying Salary" — for all local workers as a prerequisite for foreign worker access is a practical way forward.

It is estimated that 82 per cent of lower-wage employees will be covered under the PWM's latest expansion. Of the remaining 50,000 lower-wage workers, about two-thirds work in companies eligible for the new Progressive Wage Mark, which the public sector will require its suppliers to adopt. According to the Ministry of Manpower, this could raise coverage of the PWM to 94 per cent, with the balance likely to benefit from spillover effects through market forces. The upshot is that the objective of a minimum wage will be all but met.

Why not enact a minimum wage then? While there is no longer a presumption among economists that minimum wages lead to significant aggregate job losses, the employment impact on vulnerable groups may be stronger, depending on the wage level set. In Singapore, there is still a sizeable number of less-educated seniors whose employability may be affected.

The high proportion of foreigners in the workforce poses another conundrum. Extending the minimum wage to foreign workers with much lower reservation wages would raise wage costs considerably — on the other hand, limiting the minimum wage to locals would drive a further wedge between the cost of hiring locals and foreigners.

While similar concerns apply to the PWM, the tripartite consensus (where applicable) among government, employers and unions, along with customisation at the sector/occupation level, affords some assurance against local job losses. For the remaining sectors and occupations, the Local Qualifying Salary will provide a modest baseline wage for all but the smallest enterprises, and one that can be raised periodically.

NOT JUST A MATTER OF MONEY

There is also an important philosophical dimension that sets the PWM apart, which is the emphasis on skills and career progression pathways.

Rather than espouse a needs-based minimum income approach, the Government prefers to link higher pay to improved skills and productivity.

Here, the lofty ideals of PWM must confront ground realities. Tying wage increments strictly to productivity is not always feasible, as scope for productivity improvement may be constrained in some job roles or run into diminishing returns over time.

This has been recognised by the Tripartite Workgroup. While the yearly increase in PWM wage floors benefits all workers at the base, moving up the wage rungs has proved difficult for the many workers competing for limited supervisory positions. Hence, while the PWM lays down an aspirational marker, its full vision may not be easily realised.

Fortunately, PWM 2.0 does not operate alone. It builds on many years of thought and effort directed towards improving the livelihoods of lower-income Singaporeans. Interventions span upstream education and training, to downstream social support and redistribution.

The labour market, of course, plays a central role in the overall scheme — the better the outcomes from the labour market, particularly income growth and security, the less the need for downstream intervention.

In supporting lower-wage workers, PWM is complemented by Workfare, arguably the most significant enhancement to Singapore's social security framework in the past 20 years. Workfare was motivated by concern that the "working poor" was a structural rather than a cyclical problem. This became evident when the economy and broader job market began to improve from 2004 without a concurrent rise in real wages for the lower-income.

Rather than try to insulate Singaporeans from global competition by protecting jobs or enacting a minimum wage, the Government sought a structural solution that would prevent a sharp rise in applications for state assistance. Implemented in 2007, the Workfare Income Supplement (WIS) tops up the wages and CPF savings of the bottom 20 per cent of wage-earners aged 35 and above — now to be extended to those aged between 30 and 34, as announced at the National Day Rally — while the Workfare Skills Support Scheme provides additional training subsidies for lower-wage workers.

Other labour market initiatives have worked in tandem with WIS and PWM to boost local wages. Since 2010, foreign workforce tightening measures have helped to push up wages at the lower end of the skills and income distribution.

The Wage Credit Scheme incentivised firms to give wage increments to employees, while the Inclusive Growth Programme provided funding support for company projects that raised wages along with productivity. In its annual wage recommendations, the tripartite National Wages Council has regularly specified proportionately higher wage increments for lower-income workers.

With the wage disparity across occupations still relatively high in Singapore, more remains to be done. Efforts in training, productivity and job redesign, along with calibration of the foreign worker inflow, must continue in parallel with PWM and WIS, if Singapore is to succeed in improving wage outcomes for the lower-income without jeopardising business competitiveness.

SOCIETAL CONSENSUS NEEDED

Success in this endeavour will require more than just manpower rules and attendant policy levers. Higher wages will in most instances lead to higher costs which businesses will pass on, at least in part, to consumers.

While the impact can be mitigated by higher productivity and better service, a whole-of-society consensus is needed on the value of a more equitable and inclusive society. This will permeate consumer decisions on spending, business decisions on hiring and people development, and government decisions that balance economic and social objectives. PWM represents a uniquely Singaporean approach that aims to link higher wages to productivity growth and skills acquisition.

While some may prefer simpler solutions such as ringfencing certain jobs for locals or implementing a flat minimum wage, there may be value in the painstaking process of forging stakeholder consensus around a shared goal — that of inclusive progress, the foundation for a fair and cohesive society.

Foreign Manpower: Making the Global Talent Approach Work for Singapore

First published in The Straits Times on 21 September 2021

Much has been said in Parliament and the media over the past week about foreign competition in the job market. Two things are clear from this important debate.

First, Singapore must continue to welcome global talent if it is to remain a successful global city that creates good opportunities for its people. Second, a significant number of Singaporeans continue to feel deep anxiety about foreign competition for jobs. The upshot is that there is a need to find effective ways to reassure citizens and ensure that the global talent approach works well for Singapore now and into the future.

As many recognise, remaining open to global talent is necessary for Singapore to stay attractive to businesses and foreign investment, which in turn provides good jobs for Singaporeans. Regardless of the capabilities of the local workforce, there will always be shortfalls in manpower and skills that must be plugged by the foreign workforce.

Multinationals also value the flexibility to choose among the best talent available worldwide for key roles. The breadth and depth of economic activity made possible by an open economy give Singaporeans more opportunities in aggregate.

But this macro perspective, as Chua Mui Hoong pointed out ("The most worrisome fault line in Singapore", *The Straits Times*, Sept 17), is not enough to assure Singaporeans whose lived reality is competition with foreigners for jobs and promotions. Rightly or wrongly, not all Employment Pass (EP) holders are clearly better qualified for the job than locals; Singaporeans have complained of foreign bosses and recruiters favouring their compatriots over locals.

The Government has acknowledged citizens' angst. At the National Day Rally, Prime Minister Lee Hsien Loong announced that anti-discrimination legislation would be introduced to give the national fair employment watchdog, the Tripartite Alliance for Fair and Progressive Employment Practices (TAFEP), more teeth to act against errant employers. This is a significant step affirming the Government's resolve to address unfair employment practices, but it is not a panacea. Discrimination is often difficult to establish, as assessing job suitability is inherently subjective.

More importantly, the Government has been tightening the inflow of EP holders by raising the minimum salary requirements — twice in 2020 — with a higher bar for those in the financial services sector.

The Progress Singapore Party has suggested imposing an even higher qualifying salary, as well as a levy, for EP holders. Some have mooted the idea of a points-based EP system that would allow consideration of a broader set of factors including industry and firm characteristics (such as the availability of locals with relevant skills, proportion of foreign nationals) and worker characteristics (such as specific skills and work experience in Singapore).

A points-based system would enable greater selectivity of foreigners to complement the local workforce, but could also make manpower planning more challenging for firms, depending on how transparent and how complex the rules are.

While much of the discussion has rightly been on how many and who to let into Singapore, I would like to suggest there are three related dimensions to Singapore's talent approach that also merit attention.

These are: creating opportunities for Singaporeans to progress in their careers; strengthening job and social protection for citizens; and making foreigners here feel welcome. Addressing these will give Singapore the best chance of making the global talent strategy work for all.

CREATING OPPORTUNITIES FOR CAREER PROGRESSION

Singapore has invested considerably in equipping local workers with skills in order to compete for good jobs. Intensifying global competition, whether from foreigners based in Singapore or abroad, has given this added impetus.

Beyond skills, it is important that companies invest in Singaporeans and provide opportunities for career development. The SkillsFuture Leadership Development Initiative supports employers in developing or enhancing in-house leadership programmes, such as overseas assignments and cross-functional rotations, to expand the pipeline of Singaporean talent who are ready for corporate leadership roles.

The Monetary Authority of Singapore, which has been proactive in supporting financial institutions to send Singaporeans abroad to gain international experience, announced enhancements to its talent development schemes earlier this month.

It is critical to find ways to scale up such efforts across sectors and firms, such as by giving the larger employers a stronger nudge, so that Singaporeans feel they are being given fair opportunities at career development and progression.

STRENGTHENING JOB AND SOCIAL PROTECTION

Active enforcement against nationality discrimination at the workplace, backed up by the new legislation, is needed to provide baseline assurance for locals. Besides doing everything possible to help displaced workers regain employment, the Government may require new tools to help workers cope with job and income loss arising from economic volatility and business restructuring. These could include an unemployment insurance or unemployment savings scheme.

To fundamentally address the financial vulnerability many Singaporeans feel, particularly in a highly competitive, high-cost city, may require something beyond the current paradigm. A recent commentary by Nathan Gardels and Nicolas Berggruen ("Renovating democracy and the China challenge", *The Straits Times*, Sept 15) mooted the idea of "universal basic capital" — enhancing the assets of the less well-off, given that capital income is growing in relative importance to labour income in advanced economies. While Singapore practices this through significant public housing subsidies, housing assets are less easily monetised than financial assets.

The issue with distributing financial assets is that if some citizens dispose of their allotted assets for immediate consumption and fall into financial difficulty later, moral hazard arises if they are subsequently bailed out. A pragmatic alternative is a social dividend, which provides a stream of income to each citizen based on the collective capital of the nation, such as investment returns on the Government's financial reserves.

Notwithstanding the ad hoc sharing of budget surpluses with citizens from time to time, a social dividend that is paid out regularly would give Singaporeans greater peace of mind. The fiscal cost of such a dividend must be weighed against the financial assurance it would provide, which could shore up public support for policies that keep Singapore open to trade and talent.

MAKING FOREIGNERS FEEL WELCOME

Helping foreigners to feel welcome here is an important part of the equation that has perhaps received less attention than it should. While it is necessary to regulate the number of foreigners here and to provide opportunities and assurance for Singaporeans, the contributions of foreigners — whether EP, S Pass or Work Permit holders — should not go unappreciated.

The COVID-19 pandemic has proved particularly challenging for expatriates, some of whom have been away from family members for a year or longer. Many are tiring of safe distancing rules, and may look with envy at the relative freedom enjoyed in their countries of origin.

These pains will be felt until COVID-19 becomes fully endemic, but there is a good chance Singapore will retain its attractiveness to global talent in the long term, provided Singaporeans continue to welcome foreigners to our shores. In the meantime, public officers overseeing entry permits and other administrative procedures should be alert to the difficulties faced by expatriates, and exercise flexibility where possible to address legitimate needs.

While major social benefits are reserved for citizens in most countries, Singapore also applies differential pricing by residency status to a wide range of public services and amenities. This should not be taken too far, so as not to come across as excessively calculating in regard to work pass holders, who also contribute to tax revenue after all.

Also important are efforts at integrating foreigners in the community. When restrictions on social gatherings are eventually relaxed, there is much potential for locals and foreigners to bond through participation in sports and volunteerism, as well as nature, food and cultural appreciation.

Beyond one-off bonding activities, those who are new to Singapore could be invited to join interest groups with a mix of locals and foreigners who meet regularly. Expatriates come and go, but as far as possible, we would like those departing to leave with fond memories of Singapore and Singaporeans. They would then form part of Singapore's global network of "family, friends and fans", serving as informal ambassadors for Singapore overseas. This could in turn open doors for Singapore companies and citizens venturing abroad, or help to attract fresh investments and talent to Singapore.

In sum, keeping Singapore open requires careful consideration of policy levers to calibrate the number and profile of skilled foreigners entering Singapore. It also requires that Singaporeans be given assurance of fair employment and career development opportunities, along with adequate job and social protection, so that all can feel secure of their place in the nation. Finally, it is important to make foreigners here feel welcome and appreciated, and to facilitate their integration into the community. Success in these endeavours will enable locals and foreigners to thrive collectively in a gracious and welcoming global city.

Investing in Education: Returns, Risks and Career Resilience

First published in The Straits Times on 29 September 2021

Eyebrows were raised at the recent disclosure of the cost of a Yale-NUS College (YNC) liberal arts degree: tuition came to $90,800[1] a year, with the Government footing $70,300 for each Singaporean student.

This is over three times the government subsidy for an arts or science degree at the National University of Singapore (NUS). The tuition fees paid by Singaporean YNC students, at $20,500 a year, are also more than twice that paid by their counterparts in arts or science, although less than what NUS medical students fork out.

YNC's high fees may be attributed to small class sizes that allow for close interaction between students and faculty. This is the hallmark of a liberal arts education, along with exposure to a range of disciplines to foster critical thinking and the ability to approach a problem from multiple angles.

One may ask: is the amount spent on a liberal arts degree worthwhile for the individual and society? Some have gone further to question the sustainability of the traditional university model itself.

In an age where modular content can be delivered online by best-in-class instructors, going through three or four years of full-time education in a residential college may seem an inefficient way of acquiring knowledge and skills. Others contend that a university education is not just

---

[1] Unless otherwise stated, all dollar figures in the book refer to Singapore dollars.

about acquiring "hard skills", but also about "soft skills" picked up in the classroom, the opportunity to work collaboratively on projects, and the camaraderie and friendships forged during the college years.

How then should an individual choose from the smorgasbord of educational options that span the liberal arts to vocational education and professional programmes? And how should education policies and funding be directed to achieve the best outcomes for economy and society?

One's choice of education type and programme may be guided by consideration of the potential returns and risks. At the national level, there should be a portfolio of educational options to cater to the needs of the economy while accommodating different individual constraints and preferences. Future-proofing education for career resilience will allow citizens and the state to prepare for and adapt to the ever-changing market for jobs and skills.

RETURNS TO EDUCATION

The value of education, as many recognise, goes beyond pecuniary returns. It encompasses the joy of learning, the formation of character and other intangible merits that bring unique value to each individual. In weighing up educational options, most will of course give consideration to potential economic returns, to which education can contribute in several ways.

The first is the acquisition of specific skills necessary in certain professions or vocations. Examples include sporting skills, language proficiency, healthcare expertise and engineering know-how. Those with scarce skills in high demand, such as sports stars and top professionals, are amply rewarded by the market. In Singapore, the starting salaries of computer science graduates have risen rapidly in recent years, reflecting strong demand for their skills in the burgeoning digital economy.

The second is the broad training of the mind that equips the student to deal with ambiguity and complex problems that cut across boundaries. Closely related are interpersonal skills, including leadership, communication, teamwork and intercultural facility, which can be developed through student projects, presentations and class discussions. These skills may be acquired via any course of study, but are particularly emphasised in the liberal arts curriculum.

Third, friendships forged in lecture and residential halls are valuable in themselves, and can also add to one's professional network. The adage, "whom you know is as important as what you know", has proved true for many.

Finally, a university degree may serve as a signal of intellect or ability. Recruiters often use qualifications as a proxy for general ability in short-listing candidates for jobs. This may however fuel a socially wasteful paper chase, if students pursue higher education primarily for the signalling effect rather than for passion or skills that contribute to performance on the job.

RISKS

The acquisition of hard skills may open doors to technical or professional jobs, allowing the job entrant to subsequently acquire valuable industry experience. On the other hand, specific skills are susceptible to obsolescence arising from new technology, automation or changing consumer preferences. Hence, a significant investment in hard skills also comes at a risk. Some may prefer general degrees, whether in the arts, business or management, with a view to taking on jobs that do not require specific skillsets.

From the national perspective, economic and societal needs require a good spread of hard and soft skills in the workforce. It is sensible to make available a range of educational options, while ensuring there are sufficient numbers trained in critical domains, such as healthcare and engineering where indigenous capability is important. This may require directed funding and scholarships to build a pipeline of skilled manpower.

The traditional model of full-time university education confers considerable benefits beyond hard skills, and may still be a worthwhile investment for citizen and country. Concurrently, there is a need for part-time or modular courses, as well as on-the-job training, to cater to those constrained by time or finances, or who wish to pair learning with employment.

State subsidies for education and training are easily justified when aligned with national priorities, especially when grant recipients are subject to a service bond. However, higher education subsidies are often regressive, with disproportionate benefits accruing to the better-off who are more likely to pursue tertiary education. University graduates, particularly those from certain disciplines, can also expect high incomes on entering the workforce. Hence, tertiary education financing requires a judicious mix of bank loans, state grants and bursaries, as well as privately funded financial assistance.

CAREER RESILIENCE

Investment in education, like other forms of investment, is inherently risky. Both individuals and policymakers would therefore do well to think about future-proofing education for career resilience.

Establishing strong foundations in literacy and numeracy through school and college will facilitate the subsequent acquisition of close-to-market skills. For example, mathematics and quantitative reasoning underpin much of the sciences, engineering and social sciences. Foundational skills can be imparted through both academic-type programmes, as well as more hands-on, experiential pedagogy, to cater to different learning styles. There is also a place for the humanities, which speak to what it means to be human and hence can be an enduring advantage in an era of automation.

Many have found interdisciplinary exposure useful in honing a supple mind, so important for innovation and tackling "wicked" problems in the workplace and society. In Institutes of Higher Learning, this can be achieved through a core curriculum, more flexible subject combinations or complementary course pairings. For instance, engineering students may find modules on communication and business management useful in complementing the hard skills they have acquired.

While trying to predict future skills demand anywhere beyond a horizon of three to four years may be fraught, investing in "high tech" and "high touch" skills is likely a safe bet. Many jobs will entail working with technology and interacting with people, even as automation takes over routine tasks. Digital literacy will be a baseline skill necessary for all, while advanced info-communications technology skills will command a significant premium. Besides interpersonal skills, Singapore Institutes of Higher Learning are also emphasising "Asia readiness" — preparing students to tap opportunities in Asia and particularly our immediate neighbourhood, South-east Asia.

With technological advances transforming jobs and upending business models, knowledge acquired in school or college will unlikely be able to carry one through working life without a periodic refresh. Many will have to acquire new skills to pivot to new job roles in the course of their careers. Some may even consider pre-emptive "second skilling" for access to alternative career options.

At the national level, a well-oiled framework to facilitate reskilling and career transition is critical to help workers take up new opportunities as "creative destruction" reshapes the economy and job market.

In Singapore, the Government provides wage support, through Career Conversion Programmes, to companies that hire and train jobseekers for new roles. The SkillsFuture initiative supports both employer-led and self-directed learning, which can be delivered in-house by companies, or via industry training centres, tertiary educational institutions and private training providers.

Learning is a muscle that can atrophy with disuse. It is up to the individual to continually exercise this muscle in and out of the workplace. Employers and the state can help by providing the time and space, as well as funding if needed, for skills acquisition and upgrading.

Finally, one's educational and career choices should be guided by passion, to the extent practicable. The alignment of interest and aptitude can make all the difference — enabling a person to go further and achieve more in both studies and career. For the employer, this translates into greater output, productivity and job satisfaction, with attendant benefits to national competitiveness and innovation. For the individual, it is about self-actualisation — to achieve in one's work the "flow", so named by psychologist Mihaly Csikszentmihalyi, where engagement, passion and skill come together for personal and collective gain.

As Singapore's Demographics Change, So Too Must Mindsets

First published in The Straits Times on 6 October 2021

Singapore's *Population in Brief* report, released last month, revealed a record 4.1 per cent fall in total population. Foreigners accounted for much of this fall, as the COVID-19 pandemic exerted a toll on foreign employment. The resident population, too, dipped for the first time. Travel curbs kept residents away from Singapore, and fewer citizenships and permanent residencies were granted.

The data also underscored longer-term trends that preceded the pandemic, namely declining fertility and a rapidly ageing population. These have been in the making for decades. Despite all that has been said about Singapore's demographic transition, however, its implications may not have fully sunk in.

Singapore's population trajectory necessitates a re-evaluation of deeply ingrained mindsets — in particular, what it means to be a vibrant society, what it means to be Singaporean, and what it means to have a good job.

A VIBRANT, AGED SOCIETY

Mention a "vibrant society", and my mind conjures up images of young people engaged in sports and cultural activities, rather than of seniors who are in fact omnipresent in our workplaces and neighbourhoods. Such perceptions, especially if widely held, need revision.

Singapore may be a relatively young nation, but it no longer has a relatively youthful population. Gone are the days when reports extolling the efficiency of Singapore's healthcare spending were obliged to highlight Singapore's demographic advantage. Singapore's median citizen age of 42.5 years is now above those of France, Australia, China and the United States.

Singapore aspires towards economic and social vibrancy, but this can no longer be defined in terms of youthfulness: we must become a vibrant, aged society.

Over the past decade, the proportion of citizens aged 65 and above has jumped from 10.4 per cent in 2011 to 17.6 per cent in 2021, and is expected to climb to nearly one in four (23.8 per cent) by 2030. The number of senior citizens is projected to increase from slightly over 600,000 in 2021 to around 900,000 in 2030. This makes Singapore among the fastest ageing nations in the world, behind only South Korea.

The seniors of today, however, are on average better educated and in better health than their counterparts of yesteryear. They are also more likely to be actively engaged in ways that are meaningful to them, whether at the workplace, at home or in the community. "Productive longevity" is key to sustained economic and societal vibrancy even as the population greys.

Seniors who wish to continue working should be given fair opportunities to do so. Various efforts, on top of re-employment legislation, are needed: redesigning jobs to make them senior friendly, making available options for part-time and flexible work, and combating age discrimination in the job market. Retirees, too, may stay active by volunteering, pursuing hobbies or spending time with friends and family.

Infrastructure and skills are key to enabling seniors' participation in society: age-friendly buildings and public transport are critical for physical accessibility, while digital literacy is necessary for online accessibility. Lifestyle products and services catering to the silver market are also significant enablers.

The COVID-19 pandemic has put a damper on social activities, especially among older people who are at greater risk of serious illness. Once the disease is under control, however, one must hope that our seniors will be fully plugged into the community, where their participation, informed by abundant life experiences, can enrich communal life.

The passion, drive and innovation of the burgeoning silver generation can make the difference between a society brimming with verve and vitality, and one that drifts into a comfortable but listless existence. To unleash this potential, the mental compartments that separate an aged society from a vibrant one must give way, so that we can collectively reimagine Singapore as a vibrant, aged society.

A DIVERSE CITIZENRY

It is often said that one can quite easily identify a Singaporean overseas — appearance and accent are among the telltale signs. This will not be as easy going forward. Naturalised citizens will form a growing share of the Singaporean population; absent the Singlish inflections in their speech, it may take a reference to local names or places to give away their identity.

The reality is that there will be an ever-shrinking share of local-born citizens in Singapore. Efforts to attract overseas Singaporeans back to Singapore can mitigate this, but only to an extent. Even if the rate of immigration is held steady, and foreign worker inflows are carefully calibrated, the share of naturalised citizens, permanent residents and work pass holders in the total population will continue to rise.

Singaporeans must adapt to living and working among people who do not appear local, even if they hold pink identity cards. The alternative is for Singapore's population to be in continual decline, which would diminish Singapore's economic dynamism and opportunities, and would be far outside the currently envisaged population trajectory.

With an increasingly diverse Singapore tribe, the Singaporean identity can no longer be narrowly defined by the common experience of growing up here. Instead, it must be based on a shared commitment to make this island-nation a home and contribute to its success. National identity and heritage will remain the threads that stitch together the social fabric, but this fabric will acquire new blends as immigrant cultures are gradually woven in.

Culture is never static in any global city; it is continually reshaped by successive waves of immigration. Singapore, unlike states with a near-monolithic culture, is already a potpourri of ethnicities and cultures.

Since 1965, national policy has been to affirm rather than efface the country's constituent ethnic identities. This ought to make it easier to assimilate newcomers, to add new condiments to the proverbial melting pot. At a measured pace, this will adjust and enhance without overwhelming the base.

The gradual integration and assimilation of new citizens is therefore a priority. Among the children of naturalised citizens, many will grow up here, make local customs their own and contribute in their own ways to the collective experience of being Singaporean.

A BROADER RANGE OF "GOOD JOBS"

A good job in the traditional Asian, or Singaporean, paradigm, is invariably a white collar one — usually in one of the established professions, a multinational corporation or the public service. Too few aspire to be in technical or domestic services roles — as nurses, plumbers or technicians, much less as cleaners, security officers or construction workers. This poses a supply-demand conundrum. More locals are needed in essential roles that are not easily automated, so as to reduce our reliance on foreign manpower. This is for reasons of land and population constraints, national resilience, as well as to facilitate wage growth in these occupations.

Conversely, there may be too many Singaporeans hankering after a limited supply of white-collar jobs. With many more pursuing tertiary education today compared with a generation ago, the risk of underemployment is significant.

The solution must be to encourage more Singaporeans to take up jobs in the essential domestic sector. This may take more than just raising pay — work conditions and job image have to be upgraded in tandem. Firms will need to redesign jobs to make them more attractive to Singaporeans, while increasing the jobs' skills content and scope. For instance, a security officer's work can be made easier and more productive through the use of technology, while traditional retail jobs may be expanded to include online marketing responsibilities.

As Monetary Authority of Singapore Managing Director Ravi Menon recently suggested, every job ought to be professionalised. Over time, this will result in a blurring of the line between white collar and blue collar work. Even the term "Professionals, Managers and Executives" (PME), a convenient label for higher-skilled occupations, may become less relevant going forward.

There is urgency in this effort. The risk is that the demand-supply mismatch may grow in the near term, even if market forces eventually produce a new equilibrium. It may take a coordinated effort across industry, Government, unions and educators, to change the perception of what constitutes a quality job in Singapore.

Singapore's demographic trajectory is well-known, and its implications have been evident for some time now. Still, prevailing mental models about society, citizenship and jobs are hard to shake off. The more prepared citizens are to make the mental transition, the more easily Singapore as a nation can navigate the demographic transition.

What It Means to Live Well in Singapore

First published in The Straits Times on 14 October 2021, and republished in Lianhe Zaobao on 8 November 2021

How much does a family need to live comfortably in Singapore? A study, led by researchers from the National University of Singapore Lee Kuan Yew School of Public Policy and the Nanyang Technological University, has come up with the following estimates: $6,426 a month for a couple with two children aged seven to 18, and $3,218 for a single parent with a child aged two to six.

These findings are based on a research methodology known as the Minimum Income Standards approach. Focus groups comprising members of the public were asked to discuss and agree on the goods and services needed by a family for a basic standard of living, taking into account social norms and expectations.

According to the study's authors, basic needs go beyond what families require to survive; also included are items that enable "a sense of belonging, respect, security and independence". The study drew a response from the Ministry of Finance (MOF), which pointed out that the findings were highly dependent on the profile of focus group participants and the ensuing group dynamics.

MOF also highlighted, among other things, that the study should have considered lower-cost alternatives to expenditure items in the basket of needs — for instance, enrichment classes by government-run student care centres and the self-help groups, which could substitute for privately run programmes. MOF's statement affirmed continued support for those in need "through a combination of building their capacity for self-resilience, strengthening their family support, and partnering with the community for further support".

Both the household budgets study and MOF's response draw attention to vital aspects about living well in Singapore: the importance of social inclusion, the need for affordable living options, and the responsibility of individuals, families and the community.

NEED FOR SOCIAL INCLUSION

One approach to determining individual or family needs is to have experts provide input based on nutrition, healthcare and other essentials of living. While this can establish an absolute benchmark for poverty or subsistence, it is less relevant in identifying spending that appears discretionary, but is nonetheless important for social inclusion.

In Singapore, absolute poverty is much less of a concern today after decades of strong economic and income growth. However, the rising tide has lifted some boats much more than others. Inequality, the product of Singapore's economic success and global city status, matters in at least two key dimensions: its impact on social mobility, and its effect on social inclusion. For these reasons, relative poverty is also pertinent.

Many goods and services provided by the market cater to what the bulk of population can afford — for instance, casual restaurants have proliferated across suburban malls and residential estates, while hipster cafes are now common in many gentrified precincts in Singapore.

Social exclusion may arise when a child feels she cannot afford to join her friends for lunch at the mall after school, or when her classmates are comparing their holiday experiences abroad and she is left out of the conversation. There are also social norms dictating the amounts people contribute to funerals or weddings, which impinge on an individual's social respectability.

Enrichment classes speak to both social norms and social mobility. Notwithstanding the high quality of public education, many parents feel obliged to put their children through private tuition and enrichment programmes, which they view as necessary for their children to keep up or keep ahead.

The approach taken in the household budgets study, subjective as it may be, takes a crack at factoring in social norms and expectations which have a role in shaping social inclusion.

AFFORDABLE LIVING OPTIONS AND COMMON SPACES

If social inclusion is the glue holding society together, sustaining inclusivity must rank high among national policy priorities. While raising incomes and providing social transfers play a critical role in addressing the cost of living, the Government also possesses other levers that can influence affordability and hence inclusion.

For instance, government land sales affect property and rental prices. A steady supply of land adequate for residential and business needs can avert supply crunches that would drive up prices; where necessary, the authorities may also take steps to rein in property speculation. No less significant are upstream measures to influence demand, such as medical insurance reform to contain healthcare inflation.

By managing the cost of delivering public goods and services, the public sector can avoid transferring an excessive burden to the public when pricing these for cost recovery. Innovation, too, may help to cut costs. Improvements to system design and processes in public agencies and corporatised service providers have led to significant savings which may be passed on to end-users.

The point made by MOF on lower-cost alternatives is an important one. Whether provided by the public, private or people sector, affordable options for food, transport, housing, healthcare and education can hold down the cost of living for the less well-off. Take food, for instance. Supermarket house brands coexist with premium brands, catering to a spectrum of budgets and needs. Singapore's distinctive hawker fare has kept the price of cooked food relatively low for a rich country, besides engendering a shared culinary identity across socio-economic strata.

Affordable hawker food is itself the outcome of policy choices. In 2011, the Government announced that it would resume building new hawker centres after a 26-year hiatus. Social enterprise hawker centres were set up, and the subletting of hawker stalls, which had previously driven up rentals, was disallowed. The sustainability of hawker culture depends crucially on the next generation of hawkers. To this end, a work-study programme in "hawkerpreneurship" was launched to prepare young Singaporeans for a career as hawkers.

In other domains, policy decisions may likewise determine affordability. Cycling could be a viable alternative to other forms of transport if made safer and more convenient; smaller public housing units and no-frills public amenities may be welcome options for those with less financial means.

Singapore's urban planners have done well in making available free common spaces for public enjoyment, including playgrounds, parks and beaches. These are places where children from different backgrounds can mix, where families can bond over picnic dinners, and people may exercise or simply enjoy the outdoors — all without burning a hole in the pocket.

Public museums, too, are free for locals, while sports facilities can be booked at nominal fees. There is potential for these common spaces, vital for social inclusion and mixing, to be gradually expanded over time, so that Singapore will remain an inclusive home for all Singaporeans, and not just an exciting city for the well-heeled.

RESPONSIBILITY FOR SELF, FAMILY AND COMMUNITY

While recognising that socio-economic driving forces necessitate a step-up in social transfers, it is important not to let go of the spirit of personal effort and responsibility that Singaporeans are known for.

The Pioneer Generation had industry and grit in abundance; today's young have a different set of challenges, but would do well to emulate the drive and resilience of the pioneers. If there is a gap between one's income and what is required to meet basic needs, it should be reflexive to ask what one can do to reduce the gap. In today's context, this must go beyond just putting in more hours of work — managing personal finances, making prudent investments, upgrading one's skills and innovating at the workplace may all have a part to play.

In many industrialised societies, responsibility for social provision has largely passed from family and community to the state. However, there is merit in retaining in our society the "gotong royong" spirit — where members of a community look out for one another and lend mutual support.

The community is often better-placed than the state to respond quickly to local needs; social bonds are strengthened, and collective resilience enhanced, when people transcend divisions of race, religion, education and income levels, to reach out to those in need. A suite of public policies encourages responsibility for self, family and society. These include tax reliefs for topping up one's own or family members' CPF accounts for basic retirement needs; tax deductions and matching contributions for donations to charitable and social causes; and state support for social service agencies and voluntary organisations that serve the needy.

The "Many Helping Hands" approach to social service provision has resulted in instances of service gaps or overlaps, but it is sometimes necessary for the public sector to take a step back to allow the people sector to step forward.

To sustain social cohesion in Singapore, social inclusion must be prioritised; public policy should promote affordability and inclusion; and self-responsibility ought to be nurtured and reinforced. With a strong ethos of personal responsibility accompanying robust social support, Singapore can aspire to be homeland where all citizens feel they belong — a home that not only provides for their needs, but also equips and challenges them to give their best for themselves, their families and the wider community.

Ride-Hailing and Delivery Jobs Are Here to Stay — Let's Make Them Work

First published in The Straits Times on 11 March 2022

A study published last month by the Institute of Policy Studies (IPS) raised some important issues facing workers on food delivery and private-hire vehicle (PHV) online platforms.

While platform or "gig" workers enjoy flexible hours and attractive pay, the report ("Delivery, private-hire platform workers risk being trapped in poverty, precarity: Study", *The Straits Times*, Feb 28) highlighted concerns such as overwork, lack of career mobility, financial stress and inadequate retirement savings. It also pointed to workers' vulnerability to accidents, illness or unreasonable customer demands.

The challenge then is how best to address these concerns while sustaining the platform economy, which has increased access and convenience for Singapore consumers while providing income and work flexibility for gig workers.

Ride-hailing and food delivery services have become important enablers in the private transport and food & beverage sectors. The introduction of surge pricing by ride-hailing platforms has been a game-changer, cutting out long taxi queues on rainy days by improving the matching of private transport supply and demand. Food delivery services provided a lifeline for many households and food outlets during the COVID-19 "circuit breaker" in 2020. They continue to be popular today, as evident from the ubiquity of delivery riders on roads and in our neighbourhoods.

The benefits that online platforms have afforded workers are undeniable. Platform workers who put in a full day's shift have reported earnings of between $3,000 and $5,000 a month, more than some could otherwise make without specialised skills.

Others use online platforms to supplement their income, working as little or as much as they choose to meet their financial objectives. As private hire and food delivery work cannot be offshored, unlike some other freelance or IT jobs, platform workers enjoy the location-based premium of working in an affluent global city. The industry has also rationalised its incentives from the early days of intense competition for market share.

Today, the underlying demand and supply picture is clear. Platform work fills an evident market need, while also meeting increasing demand for flexible work among Singaporeans. Survey data from the Ministry of Manpower indicate that over 80 per cent of workers for whom platform work is their primary job do so out of choice rather than necessity.

In short, the platform economy is here to stay, and it is in the interest of firms and all stakeholders to find ways to improve the well-being and longer-term prospects of gig workers.

UNION REPRESENTATION, CPF SAVINGS

Let us first take a closer look at the challenges delivery and PHV workers face. As self-employed workers, they do not have the same protection given to salaried employees under the Employment Act. Furthermore, they are not entitled to union representation for collective bargaining and grievance handling, although the National Trades Union Congress has set up a Freelancers and Self-Employed Unit that provides access to insurance, training grants and seminars.

There is also concern about retirement savings, given that Singapore's social security system is based on regular Central Provident Fund (CPF) contributions. Self-employed workers are only required to contribute to MediSave — even so, some have not been contributing regularly.

In 2018, a tripartite workgroup recommended a "Contribute-As-You-Earn" (CAYE) model for the self-employed, where a MediSave contribution is required from platform intermediaries or corporate service buyers as and when a service fee is paid. The Government, as a service buyer, has piloted CAYE since 2020, making MediSave contributions easier and hassle-free for the self-employed. Besides, the Government has signalled openness to reviewing current legislation that could pave the way for union representation of freelancers.

There is scope to review the responsibilities of online platforms, and even customers, towards workers. The IPS report suggested mandating or incentivising platform companies and workers to make CPF and insurance contributions, and also implementing a rest period policy for workers who spend long hours on the road.

Appropriate regulations could help level the playing field for companies, while protecting the interests of workers. This benefits both sides, because protecting workers is ultimately in the interest of platform companies. However, rules cannot be "one size fits all", as reflected in the profile of respondents in the study. Some drive or ride as their primary job, while others do it as a side gig. They include workers with different needs and constraints, such as students, retirees, those in between jobs, as well as those with caregiving responsibilities.

Besides, two-wheel and four-wheel drivers have considerably different working conditions and so do not face the same challenges or risks. There may also be trade-offs between work protection and flexibility, which is a key motivation for many platform workers.

These are issues which the advisory committee on platform workers, set up by the Ministry of Manpower late last year, is already looking into.

For instance, the committee is considering whether platform companies should be required to make CPF contributions to support workers' housing and retirement needs. As platform work is here to stay, the committee's recommendations will be critical for this important segment of the workforce.

CREDIBLE ALTERNATIVE CAREERS?

Another concern expressed in the study is that full-time platform workers may not get as many opportunities for long-term skills acquisition and career progression (although other forms of employment may not guarantee this either). In particular, they may lack the time or motivation to invest in skills training that would enable them to secure other employment. The IPS report suggested raising awareness of government schemes that help workers reskill or find other jobs.

Although the median pay of private hire car drivers and delivery workers in 2021 was $2,000 and $1,800 respectively, some are able to earn considerably more than the median starting salary for ITE graduates ($1,720 for fresh graduates and $2,200 for post-NS graduates in 2020). For those without post-secondary education, the pay differential could be greater. Even with several years of work experience, the pay in other jobs may not match what platform work can offer.

So, in providing career guidance to workforce entrants, there is a need to identify jobs and careers that provide a credible alternative to platform work. These would be jobs that are in demand, resilient to automation and allow workers to gain skills and higher incomes over time. They could include healthcare roles such as nursing, maritime jobs for which there remains a dearth of local seafarers, and skilled occupations such as electricians, plumbers and technicians.

These roles, however, typically require much more formal training and have higher barriers to entry. Comparable jobs in retail, F&B and office administration are unlikely to match up, although the expansion of the Progressive Wage Model will see wages climb across the board over time.

In explaining their reluctance to take up skills training, full-time platform workers have cited the opportunity cost of taking time off from work without the guarantee of a new job. The prospect of training or finding employment in an unfamiliar sector may itself be daunting.

Place-and-train career conversion programmes offered by Workforce Singapore, where workers are hired first and then trained, provide job certainty for those looking for a change of career. It may also be worth enabling platform workers to try out alternative jobs with good long-term prospects, such as by providing part-time training or employment opportunities with competitive training allowances or salaries.

By strengthening worker protection and welfare, platform jobs have the potential to become quality jobs for local workers, whether as full-time or part-time work. Targeted career guidance and job matching, meanwhile, would expand career possibilities for platform workers, while optimising the nation's manpower resources for priority areas such as healthcare.

With the two-pronged approach of better worker protection and targeted career guidance, platform work could be an asset in the nation's economic and social development, as the future of work takes shape in Singapore.

Improved Meritocracy Can Focus on Skills, Training and Career Progression

First published by CNA on 15 July 2022

In launching Forward Singapore, a year-long national conversation, Deputy Prime Minister Lawrence Wong said that Singapore "cannot abandon" meritocracy despite its downsides, but can make it "more open and compassionate".

It is hard to disagree with meritocracy as a principle that upholds fair opportunities for all. But it is also evident that meritocracy can, in practice, entrench privilege and inequality.

Discussions on meritocracy tend to centre on the education system and its emphasis on academic achievement. The lower-income and less academically inclined may become casualties in a system where the more affluent can gain a head-start in life through private tuition and enrichment classes.

Various initiatives aim to give all children a good start, such as KidSTART and the Learning Support Programme, and to broaden the concept of merit to reduce emphasis on grades and consider non-academic criteria for admission to schools and tertiary institutions.

Interventions in education, however, will take time to show results. They are also not a panacea as it is hard to eliminate advantages parents can pass on to their children in both academic and non-academic domains. So to foster a more open and compassionate meritocracy, we need to look beyond the education system to the workplace and broader society, and the different roles we all play to get there.

SKILLS, TRAINING AND CAREER PROGRESSION

There must be opportunities for progression through one's working life, or what Senior Minister Tharman Shanmugaratnam has dubbed a "continuous meritocracy". Demonstrable skills, as well as learning and performance on the job, should allow each worker to go as far as he or she can without being constrained by past educational attainment. Employers can do their part by not pigeonholing employees or locking them into preset career development pathways according to education level or qualification.

This makes sense when we consider that jobs have transformed dramatically and skills require continuous refreshing. According to a 2021 PwC study, about half of Singapore workers think their job would be obsolete within five years.

While there is a place for self-directed skills upgrading, taking time off for training can seem a luxury to some workers who have job and family obligations to meet. Hence, it is important for employers to champion upgrading in skills relevant to job and business transformation, by carving out time for employee training. It makes a huge difference to motivation when workers can put to use the skills they have acquired and be rewarded for their efforts. This is the thinking behind the company training committees (CTCs), initiated by the National Trades Union Congress (NTUC), which help companies drive worker training in tandem with business transformation.

Sectoral or industry-based efforts can push the envelope further still. The Progressive Wage Model (PWM), with its sector-based wage and productivity ladders, is based on the principle of continual skills upgrading for greater productivity and pay. The idea is that no jobs should be "dead end": there must always be opportunities for personal improvement and career advancement.

VALUING THE CONTRIBUTIONS OF ALL WORKERS

By raising the incomes of lower-wage workers, PWM also supports Mr Wong's call for society to recognise the contributions of every worker, treat them with dignity and respect, and pay them well.

Mandatory PWM has been implemented in four sectors over the past eight years. As announced at the 2021 National Day Rally, it will be progressively extended to more sectors and occupations, while companies hiring foreigners will be required to pay local employees a Local Qualifying Salary (LQS) of $1,400. The expanded PWM, including the LQS requirement, will directly benefit over 8 in 10 workers in the bottom fifth of the income distribution. Forthcoming enhancements to Workfare will also raise the take-home pay of lower wage workers, including younger workers aged 30 to 34.

Wage disparities across some occupations are higher in Singapore than in the United Kingdom and other advanced economies. With the tight labour market, the pay of professionals, especially those with in-demand skills such as IT, will continue to rise. PWM plays a crucial part in ensuring that those in traditional "blue collar" work do not lag further behind. Otherwise, a two-tier economy and workforce could emerge, putting social cohesion under strain.

Raising the pay and prestige of essential service occupations such as cleaning and healthcare will also help to attract locals to such jobs and reduce Singapore's reliance on foreign manpower. This is important for a sustainable and resilient workforce.

As not all the increase in labour cost arising from PWM can be offset by productivity gains, businesses, consumers and the state will have to collectively shoulder the difference. This requires a whole-of-society consensus on the value of a more equitable society. The Government has recently announced that it will enhance the Progressive Wage Credit by funding a larger proportion of the increase in lower-wage worker salaries, to ease the transition for businesses.

WHAT WE'RE WILLING TO DO TO ACHIEVE THE KIND OF MERITOCRACY WE WANT

An open and compassionate meritocracy is in fact necessary for Singapore to remain open to trade, investment and talent from abroad.

Ultimately, Singapore can remain an open economy only if citizens across the income spectrum experience the benefits of globalisation and have an inequitable share in the fruits of economic growth. Otherwise, there is a real risk of society turning insular, just as in other advanced economies where anti-foreign sentiment has boiled over.

Besides workforce interventions, Singapore has been strengthening social safety nets including the Community Care (ComCare) schemes. To provide greater assurance for workers at a time of economic volatility, it is worth considering how to operationalise some form of unemployment relief or insurance, which could be co-funded by employers, workers and the state.

All these will however amount to higher public spending. Part of the additional revenues needed will come from higher top marginal income and property taxes introduced in Budget 2022. Further adjustments to the fiscal system may be necessary down the road, a topic that merits discussion among citizens and societal stakeholders.

Forward Singapore comes at an opportune moment for citizens from different walks of life to express their aspirations for Singapore, including the kind of meritocracy we would like to see take root here, and what we are willing to do to achieve it.

This could include a commitment to skills upgrading on the part of workers, progressive pay and employment practices on the part of employers, potential shifts in public policy, as well as a willingness on the part of citizens to accept higher costs and tax contributions, if needed, for a more equitable society.

Part B

Economic Development and Public Finance

Growing Global Champions with Roots in Singapore

First published in The Straits Times on 10 November 2021

It is, for many, a matter of national pride to have home-grown companies attain position of global dominance in their respective industries. Besides the United States, China and Japan, smaller economies have also succeeded in growing global champions such as Samsung (South Korea), Ikea (Sweden) and Nestle (Switzerland).

However, success has proved elusive for promising Singaporean companies over the years. During the early to mid-2000s, home-grown technology firm Creative Technology went toe-to-toe with Apple for supremacy in the global portable media player market, but was ultimately outmuscled by the American giant. Water treatment and environment solutions firm Hyflux won infrastructure projects in South-east Asia, China and the Middle East, but ran into financial difficulties and filed for creditor protection in 2018.

Of late, the digital economy has thrown up opportunities for "unicorns" to emerge. Singapore-based Grab has grown from a ride-hailing app to a regional behemoth with interests spanning food delivery to digital payments. Sea, the parent company of e-commerce player Shopee and games developer Garena, has seen its stock price surge since its US listing in 2017, becoming South-east Asia's most valuable public company.

One may ask: Does this represent a turning point for Singapore's long-held ambitions to grow global companies? What new opportunities have emerged, and how can Singapore capture value from the success of its firms?

THE QUEST FOR 'LOCAL TIMBER'

Multinational corporations (MNCs) have been the driving force behind Singapore's economic development since the 1960s, providing jobs, technology, organisation and market access. While MNCs remain a vital part in Singapore's enterprise ecosystem, the desire to grow large local enterprises has gained impetus through the years. A perennial concern is that footloose MNCs may relocate their operations to major markets and production centres elsewhere. Many have called for Singapore to "grow our own timber", by nurturing local champions alongside foreign heavyweights.

A succession of national economic planning committees has affirmed this intent. The 2010 Economic Strategies Committee set a target of doubling the number of "globally competitive companies" — local firms with revenues exceeding $100 million — from around 500 in 2009 to 1,000 by 2020.

In its 2017 report, the Committee on the Future Economy articulated plans to help high-growth enterprises scale up and internationalise through targeted support, including access to networks, mentors, technology and financing. Historically, Temasek-linked companies that grew out of former state enterprises have found it easier to venture overseas, being able to leverage their track record, expertise and financial strength to make overseas acquisitions and establish themselves abroad. These include DBS Bank, Singtel and CapitaLand, which have a significant international presence, particularly in Asia.

Smaller players could turn to SPRING Singapore and International Enterprise Singapore — now merged to form Enterprise Singapore — for support. Over the years, a panoply of grants has been offered for capability building, innovation and internationalisation, along with an array of loan and equity financing schemes.

Yet some in the business and academic community have called for more to be done for small and medium enterprises (SMEs). Among the litany of grouses: onerous grant application processes; an unlevel playing field vis-à-vis MNCs, which enjoy larger tax benefits and the pick of talent; and foreign competitors that are backed to the hilt by their respective governments.

What does it take to succeed, and what opportunities are on the horizon? Before going global, many companies first establish themselves domestically, sinking roots in a conducive business substrate. Singapore generally scores well on business-friendly laws and regulations, good infrastructure and trade connectivity. Considerable investment has been poured into research and development, with an emphasis on bringing technology to market.

Beyond grants and tax incentives, various ideas have been floated to plug perceived gaps in enterprise support. These include a dedicated SME bank to increase access to finance, as well as an export-import (EXIM) bank or export credit agency to lower the cost of cross-border finance. Some have also suggested a larger role for government procurement to generate "lead demand" for local companies, so as to help them establish a track record.

Also important is a supply of "patient capital" to nurture promising firms, particularly those with a long gestation period before generating positive cashflow. Under the Co-Investment Programme (CIP) set up in 2010, the Government co-invests, alongside Temasek Holdings and private equity funds, in promising Singapore-based firms. These span diverse sectors including healthcare (Eagle Eye Centre), engineering solutions (Hope Technik), gaming hardware (Razer) and sanitary ware (Rigel).

CIP-supported firms have found Temasek's involvement useful not just for capital, but also to leverage the Temasek brand and network. Private equity fund managers add value to investee firms' management teams through mentoring by experienced business leaders. Recent developments in financing, digitalisation and sustainable development hold considerable promise for local enterprises looking to conquer regional and global markets.

First, the world is awash with capital in search of returns. Venture and private equity funds are on the prowl for suitable investments, with Southeast Asia a happy hunting ground. Firms with promising technology and business models can tap on a range of financing options to spread their wings abroad.

Temasek's newly established investment platform, 65 Equity Partners, will complement the existing Co-Investment Fund by offering private financing for larger local firms (valued between US$1 billion and US$5 billion) with regional or global aspirations. Meanwhile, special purpose acquisition companies (SPACs) are gaining prominence as an alternative to traditional Initial Public Offerings for firms that are considering going public.

Besides capital, Singapore companies need people to spearhead overseas expansion, whether Singaporeans who are prepared to live and work abroad, or foreigners with in-depth knowledge of their home markets. While local enterprises continue to face stiff competition for manpower from MNCs and the public sector, some have found ways to attract and develop the talent they need. Companies may tap the SkillsFuture Leadership Development Initiative to send local employees on overseas assignments. They may also recruit foreign students graduating from local tertiary educational institutions to support their expansion in South-east Asia and beyond.

Second, a surge in digital services, including e-commerce and e-payment, has made it easier for companies to tap regional and global markets for sales from the get-go. A report by Google, Temasek and Bain released in November 2020 found that as many as 40 million people in six South-east Asian countries came online for the first time last year, raising the number of Internet users to 400 million or nearly 70 per cent of the population in those countries.

Under the Infocomm Media Development Authority's SMEs Go Digital programme, SMEs can come aboard e-commerce platforms to sell overseas. Companies with their own platforms, user base and data may be able to scale rapidly across geographies and service offerings, as Grab and Sea have demonstrated.

Building on Singapore's network of Free Trade Agreements, the Government has negotiated Digital Economy Agreements with Chile, New Zealand and Australia. Other agreements are in the pipeline, paving the way for firms to grow their digital trade and e-commerce footprint.

Finally, the global momentum towards clean energy and environmental sustainability will present local companies with opportunities to take the lead in this space. There are already various national initiatives to promote green finance and help enterprises build sustainability capabilities. This is an area that holds much promise for the future, and is well worth the investment.

HOW CAN SINGAPORE CAPTURE VALUE?

National pride aside, growing Singaporean multinationals is not an end in itself. It is worth noting that despite its impressive stable of global conglomerates, South Korea has a lower median income than Singapore. Evidently, it takes much more than highly productive national champions to achieve high incomes and inclusive economic growth for citizens.

Even if local enterprises succeed in becoming global champions, there is no guarantee that the value they create will accrue to Singapore. Some will be acquired by foreign investors or multinationals. Regardless of ownership, companies may decide to locate production and operations in countries with lower production costs and larger markets.

In the information and communications technology sector, for instance, programmers in Vietnam and Indonesia can deliver quality services at a fraction of the cost of their Singapore counterparts. Research and development, too, may migrate to countries with an abundant supply of research scientists and engineers.

Ultimately, the same factors that make Singapore attractive to foreign investment will also anchor home-grown companies here. Of vital importance is the enterprise ecosystem that spans start-ups, SMEs and large enterprises, both local and foreign. The concentration of capital and talent in Singapore creates economies of agglomeration, investing Singapore with a competitive advantage that is "sticky" or resilient despite our higher cost.

Innovation networks play a particularly important role, with successful entrepreneurs in turn becoming angel investors and mentors. These networks will take time to build up in Singapore, and success is by no means guaranteed.

It is necessary for our local champions to derive value from Singapore, whether through networks, trust or reputation for excellence. By establishing headquarters in Singapore and performing high-value activities here, they can create good jobs and contribute to the enterprise ecosystem.

Although Razer and Sea are listed in Hong Kong and New York respectively, they are ramping up their presence in Singapore: Razer opened its $100 million South-east Asia headquarters in Singapore last month (Oct), with plans to boost staff strength here from 600 to around 1,000 by 2023, while Sea is leasing new office space here as it pursues business growth.

Home-grown global companies will naturally perform many activities abroad, but Singapore will gain only if they remain rooted here, deriving value from their home base and in turn contributing value to the economy and people.

Getting More Bang from the R&D Buck

First published in The Straits Times on 30 November 2021

Singapore has built up a strong research and development (R&D) base, thanks to sustained investment over many years. A total of $25 billion will be committed to research, innovation and enterprise under the government's latest five-year plan (RIE 2025) from 2021–2025.

The benefits derived from R&D have also been substantial, such as in the national effort to combat COVID-19. The scaling-up of COVID-19 testing capability here owes much to locally developed test kits. Diagnostic innovations from Singapore laboratories were quickly translated to clinically validated, mass-manufactured test kits through close collaboration between research institutions, healthcare providers and local medical technology manufacturers.

In the burgeoning field of Artificial Intelligence (AI), just this month a new public AI programme was launched as part of a concerted effort to harness AI for social and economic good. The National AI Programme in Finance is a collaboration between Singapore-based banks and local fintech companies that includes an industry-wide AI platform — dubbed NovA! — which will help financial institutions assess firms' environmental impact and risks. This is especially relevant in the wake of COP-26.

With Singapore's R&D base maturing, the challenge now is to extract greater value from the considerable public investment in R&D.

How can this be achieved? Sustaining a strong foundation in basic research, strengthening pathways to translate research findings into commercial opportunity, and facilitating the deployment of technology and R&D solutions will be critical.

AIMS AND OUTCOMES

Broadly speaking, public R&D spending serves to address national or societal priorities, derive economic gain, and enhance scientific or academic reputation. As a small country accounting for a small fraction of global research spending, Singapore cannot excel at everything, and must be selective about its research priorities.

Solutions to national needs may be developed through R&D or purchased from abroad. In deciding whether to "build" or "buy": First, does the research address issues particularly important to Singapore, requiring solutions that are not commercially available elsewhere? Second, can Singapore realise economic gains from being a first mover, for example, by enabling Singapore firms to capture market share through superior products and services or by licensing intellectual property? Third, is Singapore well-placed to be a global leader in a particular domain?

Singapore's urban living challenges have impelled development of expertise in urban solutions and sustainability. For instance, Singapore's water needs have spawned a thriving water industry with 180 companies and over 20 water research centres. The rapidly ageing population, likewise, has spurred research into ageing, along with the rollout of products and services catering to seniors. This suggests the possibility of synergies between research excellence and impact in terms of economic and societal outcomes.

Over the years, the research generated by our universities, research institutes and hospitals has grown in volume and quality. Singapore was ranked eighth globally in the 2021 World Intellectual Property Organization (WIPO) Global Innovation Index and second in the 2021 Bloomberg Innovation Index.

However, the efficiency of Singapore's R&D investments — how much innovation output a country is getting for its inputs — lags behind other countries: the Global Innovation Index ranked Singapore first on input but a mere 13th on output. The persistent gap between Singapore's innovation input and output performance has added impetus to get more out of every dollar spent on R&D.

BACK TO BASICS

With the growing emphasis on R&D commercialisation, it is important not to neglect investment in basic research, which underpins Singapore's status as an R&D hub and talent magnet, and can lead to positive spillovers and serendipitous applications. Basic science is the foundation of the entire value chain in research, innovation and enterprise. Funding excellence in basic research is an investment in talent. Leading scientists in turn attract companies, investment and other research and entrepreneurial talent.

A strong R&D base also increases the absorptive capacity for technology, enabling countries and firms to be smart buyers and integrators of technology. So it is appropriate that a third of Singapore's $25 billion RIE funding has been committed to basic research. It may, however, take time for value to be realised. In the area of drug discovery, for instance, Singapore is finally seeing results from investments made years ago, with cancer drug candidates now moving into clinical trials and commercialisation.

The journey from scientific discovery to application is often circuitous. It may be difficult at the outset to identify commercial uses, while discoveries made in one domain could find unexpected applications elsewhere. Hence, Singapore needs to be embedded in upstream and downstream research in various focus areas to have the best chance of making timely discoveries and capturing value.

NO LONGER LOST IN TRANSLATION

The potential for economic value capture is greater if there are pathways to translate research discoveries into commercial applications. There is scope to bring to market more of the research done in Singapore's universities and research institutes. The Experimental Drug Development Centre, opened in 2019, offers a conduit for high potential drug candidates to realise commercial as well as clinical outcomes, with a focus on diseases prevalent in Asia. Also launched in 2019, the Target Translation Consortium coordinates early-stage drug discovery efforts across academic institutions, healthcare institutions and government agencies.

Where innovation is industry-led, there is a high likelihood of successful commercial applications. Last month, ST Engineering announced a new research collaboration model (Research Translation @ ST Engineering) that brings together engineers and researchers from the company, universities and A*STAR in a common collaborative space. Its aim is to spur customer-centric R&D, translating laboratory research to prototype development and the rollout of commercial products.

Singapore's start-up ecosystem, too, is playing a growing part in demand-pull innovation. For instance, start-ups have been working with larger corporates to develop market solutions under thematic open innovation calls, in partnership with public agencies and research outfits. While the start-up space has been dominated by consumer-facing enterprises, "deep technology" start-ups in areas such as advanced manufacturing, health and sustainability are emerging, with strong potential to leverage R&D and intellectual property for competitive advantage.

THE PUBLIC SECTOR'S ROLE IN TECH DEPLOYMENT

Besides the private sector, the public sector may also generate demand for R&D. This requires sufficient focus on technology and innovation within public agencies, notwithstanding the many pressing issues vying for management attention. Innovation, after all, could yield solutions to public sector challenges such as sustainability, productivity and safety.

There may be a place for "Big, Hairy, Audacious Goals" such as to lower the ambient temperature in residential areas to a target range, or to achieve energy self-sufficiency in waste water treatment by a set date. A clearly articulated target could serve to mobilise R&D efforts across a range of research domains and institutions.

To be able to deploy technology in operations effectively, public agencies must also develop "ops-tech" capability. One way is by recruiting and developing scientists and engineers, not just for in-house R&D,

but also as smart buyers and technology "brokers" who can advise management on how to develop, procure and implement technological solutions.

Recent years have seen efforts to strengthen public sector engineering expertise and build capabilities in emerging technologies. In particular, the Government Technology Agency (GovTech) is spearheading the transformation of public service delivery through technologies such as AI and machine learning, along with data science and analytics. This entails working closely with public agencies, citizens and businesses to understand user needs and how best to address them.

Sometimes, regulations may pose a barrier to the deployment of new technology. The challenge for regulators is how to manage risk while giving sufficient leeway for the testing of new technologies and business models. In the area of financial technology, for example, the Monetary Authority of Singapore's "regulatory sandbox" allows for experimentation with innovative financial products and services. Financial institutions or fintech players can market test innovations within a well-defined space and duration. Safeguards are in place to contain the consequences of failure and preserve the integrity of the financial system.

The proof of the pudding is whether regulatory frameworks permit the timely deployment of new technologies at scale, so that the full benefits of innovation can be reaped. It is, of course, possible to wait for a technology to be fully mature before allowing its adoption, but Singapore may then miss out on a first-mover advantage, or even fall behind the curve.

Innovators may require a degree of regulatory certainty before proceeding to the next stage in developing a new technology or product. What may be helpful is for regulatory agencies to articulate clear targets and obligations, such as a commitment to allow autonomous vehicles on the roads when the accident rate in trials is below half the human driver rate. This could open the door to faster innovation at scale.

CAPTURING GREATER VALUE

Over successive national science plans, public expenditure on R&D has grown substantially, in tandem with economic growth. The $25 billion budget for RIE 2025 is up from $19 billion for RIE 2020 and $16 billion for RIE 2015. Public R&D spending has been pegged at around 1 per cent of GDP, putting Singapore on par with other small advanced economies such as Denmark and Sweden.

While Singapore's research, innovation and enterprise ecosystem has already generated considerable economic and social impact, there is scope to capture greater value still from public investment in R&D. Harnessing the full potential of our R&D talent, infrastructure and institutions will be central to Singapore's efforts to survive and thrive in the post-pandemic world.

Why the Need to Raise the GST Now?

First published by CNA on 23 January 2021

When then Finance Minister, Mr Heng Swee Keat, announced the Goods and Services Tax (GST) hike in 2018, he said it was necessary to strengthen Singapore's revenues, given increases in recurrent spending on healthcare, security and other social needs. He said the GST would be raised from 7 per cent to 9 per cent sometime between 2021 and 2025, depending on the state of the economy and public finances, and likely earlier rather than later within this period.

The GST hike was held off last year as Singapore grappled with the economic fallout of COVID-19. However, Prime Minister Lee Hsien Loong indicated in his recent New Year message that the Government will have to "start moving" on the hike in Budget 2022 as Singapore emerges from the pandemic.

Several questions may come to mind. First, what exactly is driving the increase in public expenditure that necessitates a higher GST? Second, can Singapore tap other revenue streams in lieu of raising the GST? Third, what impact will a higher GST have on lower-income Singaporeans, particularly as inflation picks up?

AGEING DEMOGRAPHIC AMONG THE KEY DRIVERS

Since the GST was last raised in 2007, and even before the pandemic, public expenditure has grown significantly. Between 2007 and 2019, government spending rose from $33 billion to $75 billion a year. Social spending nearly tripled over this period. Healthcare expenditure, in particular, soared from $2.2 billion to $11.3 billion.

The surge in healthcare spending comes as no surprise, given Singapore's demographic transition. By some estimates, Singapore is ageing faster than any other country bar South Korea in terms of the projected increase in senior population share between now and 2050. By 2030, By 2030, nearly one in four citizens here will be aged 65 and above, up from about one in eight in 2015. They are three to four times more likely to be admitted to hospital compared with younger Singaporeans, and once admitted, typically stay for close to twice as long. On average, a senior receives more than six times the annual public healthcare subsidies received by those under 65.

Costs have also risen with advances in medical technology and better standards of care. For instance, the discovery of targetable genes has led to new, more expensive cancer therapies. Surgical procedures such as total knee replacement are also becoming more prevalent.

To be sure, there is scope to achieve greater efficiency in healthcare spending. Insurance reform, including the new co-payment requirement for Integrated Shield Plan riders, would help, as would the rebalancing of care between acute hospitals and step-down facilities. That said, Singapore's healthcare efficiency is high by international standards: in 2020, Singapore topped the Bloomberg Health-Efficiency Index, which was adjusted to include the impact of COVID-19.

SPENDING NEEDED TO KEEP INEQUALITY IN CHECK

Greater spending is also needed to sustain social mobility and keep inequality in check. For instance, the Workfare Income Supplement (WIS) and Silver Support schemes have been significantly enhanced since their introduction to provide greater support for lower-income workers and retirees.

Public spending on early childhood education and lifelong learning has also risen considerably. Such investment is important in giving our young the best start in life, and to help citizens in the workforce continually refresh their skills to keep up with changing market demands.

As collective aspirations grow, the Government has taken on a greater role in allocating resources for programmes and services that benefit all Singaporeans, rather than just leaving this to the market.

WHERE DOES REVENUE COME FROM?

To meet rising expenditure needs, the Government has expanded and diversified revenue streams over the years. Property taxes were made more progressive in 2010 and 2013, while higher tax rates were imposed on luxury cars from 2013. Changes in personal income taxes that took effect in 2012 and 2017 increased the tax contributions from high-income earners.

The most significant growth in revenues has come from the introduction of the Net Investment Returns Contribution (NIRC) framework in 2009, and its expansion to include Temasek Holdings in 2016. With this, the revenue from Singapore's investment returns grew to $17 billion in 2019 and now accounts for about a fifth of the government's annual budget.

In the coming years, several factors may buoy revenues. Stamp duty collection is likely to remain elevated amid the property boom, while the carbon tax rate is set to increase. Some have suggested that the proposed global minimum corporate tax rate could also lead to higher corporate tax receipts in Singapore. Finally, the Government has passed legislation enabling it to borrow to fund long-term infrastructure development, easing the pressure on the fiscal system.

MORE IS STILL NEEDED

These developments, however, do not preclude the need to seek other sources of revenue. Asset tax revenues rise and fall with the market, while higher carbon tax receipts will only partly offset the increasing cost of climate mitigation and adaptation — measures projected to cost $100 billion.

The impact of a global minimum corporate tax rate on Singapore's fiscal position will depend on details yet to be worked out, and it is even possible that Singapore may lose tax revenue to other jurisdictions. The Government has also indicated that it will not borrow to fund recurrent expenditure as a matter of principle, so that the burden of spending is not transferred to future generations.

While there are calls for Singapore to tap the past reserves for more income, their investment returns are already Singapore's largest source of public revenue, larger than any single tax. The appropriate balance between extracting more for current spending and growing the principal to benefit future generations is ultimately a political judgement call.

GST A STABLE TAX

Among potential sources of additional revenue, the GST is attractive in that it is an efficient tax, with a relatively low cost of collection and administration. Compared with income and wealth taxes, GST revenue is less correlated with business cycles and therefore more stable and predictable, while being harder to circumvent through tax planning.

This is why most countries, developed and developing, have adopted a GST or value-added tax, many at rates higher than Singapore's. The drawback is that GST is a regressive tax — the less well-off tend to pay more GST relative to their incomes. However, it is important to assess a fiscal system in its totality.

The regressive impact of the GST is offset by progressive income taxes and significant fiscal transfers including WIS, Silver Support and the GST Voucher scheme. In fact, the expansion of these transfers has increased the overall progressivity of the system over the past two decades.

CUSHIONING THE IMPACT, SEEKING PUBLIC BUY-IN

Still, there are concerns that the GST increase will raise costs at a time when inflation is gathering pace globally. Prices here are rising in tandem with the cost of oil, food and raw materials; the Government projects a core inflation rate of 1 to 2 per cent this year, higher than in the past two years.

The $6 billion Assurance Package, announced in Budget 2020, will offset the impact of a higher GST by five years for most Singaporeans and by 10 years for the lower-income group. In designing this support, the Government could seek to address near-term cost pressures in addition to the impact of the GST increase.

Besides addressing costs, two other factors are critical to public buy-in for the GST hike. First, the Government must be seen to be exercising prudence in public expenditure — whether in infrastructure development, economic programmes or social spending. Otherwise, evidence of wastage or extravagance would weaken the case for raising GST.

Second, the overall fiscal system must remain equitable, with the better-off contributing their fair share of taxes. To this end, the Government may want to consider strengthening the progressivity of asset taxes further or introducing new forms of wealth taxes in due course. However, there are limits to how much additional revenue such taxation could net without jeopardising Singapore's attractiveness as a business and wealth hub.

A GST increase is never an easy sell. It will cause some unhappiness, but this long-awaited move is part of the broader effort to help shore up Singapore's revenues, giving the nation the wherewithal to tackle the challenges that lie ahead.

Let's Bite the Bullet on Taxes and Manpower Rules

First published in The Straits Times on 11 February 2022

Singapore is still emerging from the COVID-19 pandemic, the nation's greatest social and economic dislocation in the past half-century. So it may not seem the time to raise taxes or tighten foreign worker policies. However, Budget 2022 — to be delivered on Feb 18 — is a timely opportunity to set in motion plans for the country's long-term future.

Notwithstanding the tribulations of the past two years, Singapore's economy and labour market have come through better than expected. After contracting by 5.4 per cent in 2020, the economy rebounded by 7.2 per cent last year, and is forecast to expand by 3–5 per cent this year. The incidence of retrenchment in 2020 was lower than during the SARS outbreak and Global Financial Crisis (GFC) of 2008–09, while the quarterly resident unemployment rate remained below previous crisis peaks in 2003 and 2009. The resident employment rate, meanwhile, has already risen above pre-pandemic levels.

Now that economic recovery is on a firmer footing, relief measures should be targeted at just the worst-hit sectors such as aviation and tourism. Priority should go to building a more resilient and sustainable fiscal system, social support framework and workforce. In doing so, the Government will need to carefully consider how to address the understandable concerns of households and businesses.

GOODS AND SERVICES TAX (GST) AND CARBON TAXES — EASING THE TRANSITION

Key announcements expected in Budget 2022 include details of the planned GST hike from 7 to 9 per cent, and the trajectory of carbon tax increases between 2024 and 2030. These are necessary moves for fiscal and environmental sustainability respectively. The former is part of a broader effort to strengthen the Government's revenue base to fund growing operating expenses, particularly healthcare, as the population ages. The latter will give companies a stronger impetus to reduce emissions, helping Singapore to transition more quickly to a low-carbon economy.

A potential spanner in the works is the rise in inflation, propelled by a confluence of factors including global supply disruptions and robust demand. Some have called for the Government to defer the GST increase or exempt certain items so as to avoid adding to cost pressures faced by businesses and households.

However, there is urgency in rebuilding public finances within the current term of government. To contain inflation, the Monetary Authority of Singapore has already tightened monetary policy in January, and could take further action at its upcoming policy review in April if needed.

On the timing of the GST increase, a possible middle ground would be to implement the hike in two steps — perhaps a year apart — rather than in a single bound. This would diffuse the impact on consumer and business confidence, taking into consideration ongoing economic uncertainty and the risk of inflationary expectations.

For both tax increases, government support will be critical to ease the transition. The impact of the carbon tax on industry can be offset by public grants for companies to invest in energy efficiency and low-carbon technologies. Lower- and middle-income households are likely to receive additional utility rebates to help with higher electricity and gas prices. One perception that needs addressing is that while revenue collection is permanent and comprehensive, flowback and offsets to businesses and households are often short-lived and contingent.

So it is notable that the Government will be enhancing the GST Voucher scheme, a permanent GST offset package comprising cash, MediSave top-ups and utilities rebates for lower-income households.

Furthermore, the previously announced $6 billion Assurance Package will offset the impact of the GST increase on lower- and middle-income households for 10 and five years respectively.

However, as Straits Times editor-at-large Han Fook Kwang pointed out in his recent commentary (*The Straits Times*, Feb 6), offset measures will need to be comprehensive enough to cover all affected groups, and flexible enough to adjust to changing circumstances. Without this, fiscal resilience may come at the cost of social resilience.

STRENGTHENING SOCIAL SUPPORT

Strengthening the social support system is among the Budget priorities outlined by Finance Minister Lawrence Wong. This would give Singaporeans greater assurance to deal with life's uncertainties, especially in view of economic volatility and the high cost of living in a global city.

Financial support for the unemployed has so far focused on the needy who have little savings and no other means of support. However, a joint National Trades Union Congress (NTUC) and Singapore National Employers Federation (SNEF) taskforce on professionals, managers and executives (PMEs) has recommended providing supplementary income relief to who are willing but unable to find employment.

Singapore is unlikely to go as far as the Nordic countries in providing universal welfare support, as this is typically financed by substantial taxes on the middle-class, which Singapore has tried to avoid. Still, the growing aspiration for higher wages and stronger social support will lead to higher costs that society will have to shoulder.

WEALTH TAXES — A MATTER OF EQUITY

For reasons of equity, the better-off will have to do their part. Wealth taxes can help to temper inequality, particularly as asset prices have soared in Singapore and around the world. Prime Minister Lee Hsien Loong has said that the Government supports wealth taxes in principle, while noting that they are not easy to implement.

So far, Singapore has focused on taxing property rather than other forms of wealth, given the potential for tax avoidance and capital flight.

The Government could consider adjusting the existing framework of property taxes and stamp duties, such as by making them more progressive, or introducing taxes on other assets and transactions if ways can be found to mitigate the downside risks.

Such taxes ought to target the highly affluent while minimising the incidence on the broad middle class, even if the amount of revenue that can be raised this way is constrained by the comparative ease with which the rich can move capital from one country to another. It is worth noting that fiscal sustainability requires both robust revenue streams as well as efficient public spending. The Singapore Government prides itself on the latter, but it is still possible to do better, particularly in managing expenditure on big ticket items such as infrastructure and IT system development.

FOREIGN MANPOWER INTAKE SHOULD BE SELECTIVE AND SUSTAINABLE

Changes to foreign manpower policies may also be on the cards in Budget 2022. Comprising about a third of Singapore's workforce, foreigners across the skills spectrum play a critical role in sustaining a diversified and competitive economy. However, their numbers cannot increase indefinitely, even as manpower demand grows and local workforce growth tapers off. Relying too heavily on foreign workers also blunts incentives to improve productivity and develop the local workforce, hampering job and workforce transformation.

Restrictions on travel have seen foreign employment plunge over the past two years, but this can quickly reverse as borders reopen and economic growth picks up. It may seem an odd time to prioritise policy tightening when many businesses are still crying out for manpower. However, the experience of the past two decades suggest the need to act pre-emptively.

In the four years between 2005 and 2009, the number of foreigners in the population jumped by 57 per cent as the economy recovered from a period of slow growth in the early 2000s. This resulted in a slew of policy measures to moderate the inflow of foreign workers, beginning in 2010.

Despite yearly updates to foreign worker levies, quotas and qualifying salaries, it took several years to rein in foreign worker growth.

As Singapore emerges from the COVID-19 pandemic, there may well be another surge in foreign manpower demand. Social and economic needs are fast expanding, and Singapore remains attractive as a business and talent hub for reasons of connectivity, stability and liveability.

Greater effort to localise jobs will be critical for long-term workforce resilience. So it is timely to update policies to ensure that the intake of foreign workers is sustainable and complements the local workforce. The Government has already telegraphed in Parliamentary speeches last year that updates to Employment Pass (EP) and S Pass policies are in the works. This could mean using existing policy levers, or refining the policy framework itself.

A potential change to the EP framework could entail adopting a points-based system, as suggested by the PME taskforce. This would allow other factors besides salary to be taken into account in determining EP eligibility, such as the diversity of a company's workforce or whether a worker possesses specific skills that are in short supply here. There may also be merit in considering a worker's years of experience in Singapore, which would help firms retain long-serving employees who might otherwise be forced to leave as salary thresholds are periodically raised.

While a points-based system would enable greater selectivity of EP holders, it should be kept as simple and transparent as possible. Otherwise, it could complicate companies' workforce planning and reduce the ease of doing business here.

In updating foreign manpower policies, the Government must continue to emphasise that Singapore is not turning insular, as remaining open to international talent, innovation and capital will be critical for the nation's long-term competitiveness.

It will take a judicious balance between addressing immediate needs and long-term priorities if Singapore is to succeed in building a post-pandemic future with confidence and solidarity. With so much at stake, Budget 2022 is poised to be a watershed in the nation's progress.

Greater Social Spending and Redistribution Rest on Economic Growth and Government Prudence

First published by CNA on 19 February 2022

The Singapore Government's Budget 2022 was as much an articulation of shared values as it was of the policy directions and details which the Government has set out.

"We want every Singaporean to know and feel that he or she has a stake in our society ... We want to uphold that sense of obligation to each other, and strengthen the assurance that, whatever the challenges we face, we will always have each other's back," Finance Minister Lawrence Wong said on Friday (Feb 18), speaking in Parliament.

What came across unequivocally in Mr Wong's speech was the vision of an inclusive society with a strong social compact. In many countries, the gap between the haves and the have-nots in recent years has fuelled tensions and populism, dividing societies. For Singaporeans looking to see how the Government will keep inequality in check and help the most vulnerable, it was useful that the Budget underscored the importance and urgency of keeping ours a society where all can aspire to a better life.

Singapore is fortunate to be able to tap on the Government's Past Reserves to fund a significant portion of its COVID-19 support measures over the past two years — to help workers hold on to jobs and keep households afloat.

However, the country's rapidly growing social expenditure needs over the long term, in healthcare as well as in social support and redistribution, still require recurrent revenue streams that are robust and resilient.

GROWTH IS NEEDED TO SUPPORT THOSE WHO HAVE LESS IN SOCIETY

Can we find the money to do all this? Much depends on the health of our economy. Economic vibrancy is vital to generate needed revenues for this social spending and redistribution. A 2009 study by the Ministry of Finance found a strong correlation (0.92) between tax revenues and GDP over the period 1998 to 2007.

Besides macroeconomic stability and a conducive business environment, continued investment in infrastructure, skills and capabilities is needed to grow the economy. So Mr Wong's announced funding to upgrade Singapore's digital capabilities, strengthen local enterprises and invest in training will be critical to generate corporate and personal income, on which tax revenues depend.

Notwithstanding these efforts, the economic pie is unlikely to expand as fast as in previous decades. Now that Singapore is a high-income economy that is closer to the frontier of technology and productivity, the scope for catch-up growth is lower.

When Singapore was a young nation, a rising tide lifted all boats. Today, as a maturing society with wealth and socio-economic advantages accumulated over several generations, fiscal redistribution will play a larger part in tempering inequality and sustaining social mobility through education and other social investments.

HOW THE TAX SYSTEM IS EVOLVING TO SUPPORT REDISTRIBUTION

Some ask if our tax system can be reviewed to give more to those in need. Indeed, Singapore's tax system has evolved over the years to support redistribution while keeping the overall tax burden low. Everyone contributes something in taxes, with the better-off contributing more.

The latest tax changes are part of this evolution. Though Budget 2022 stands out as one that has made a further, significant shift towards greater progressivity in both income and asset taxes, past Budgets — particularly those in 2010, 2013 and 2015 — have seen moves to enhance progressivity in income and asset taxes and tax reliefs.

With GST set to increase, there was much pre-Budget speculation on what new forms of wealth taxes might be on the cards and whether estate duty, abolished in 2008, would return. The Government opted instead to work within the existing framework of taxes on residential properties and luxury cars, given the practical difficulty of fairly assessing a person's net wealth, as well as the mobility of other forms of wealth across borders.

It also raised the top marginal personal income tax rate for those earning over $500,000. This increase in personal income taxes for the top 1.2 per cent of wage earners is expected to raise about $170 million in additional revenues each year. This builds on the personal income tax hike announced in Budget 2015, which affected the top 5 per cent of wage earners with a projected gain of $400 million.

The residential property tax revisions at Budget 2022 meanwhile have a broader catchment, and are estimated to net $380 million more a year, with the top 7 per cent of owner-occupied properties and all non-owner occupied properties affected. By contrast, the last revision to property taxes announced in Budget 2013 saw the top 1 per cent of owner-occupied properties and top one-third of non-owner-occupied properties incur higher taxes, while the 0 per cent property tax band for owner-occupied properties was increased to cover more homes, netting an estimated revenue gain of $53 million to the Government.

AUGMENTING SOCIAL SUPPORT

Over the past decade, increasing social transfers have seen a trend decline in Singapore's Gini coefficient, a measure of income inequality. After accounting for taxes and transfers, the Gini coefficient based on household income per household member in 2021 was the lowest on record apart from 2020 when there was exceptional pandemic-related social support.

Budget 2022 takes a further step in this direction by augmenting existing pillars of social support. Lower-wage workers stand to benefit from the expansion of progressive wages and the enhancement of the Workfare Income Supplement. A new Progressive Wage Credit Scheme (PWCS) to co-fund the wage increases of lower-wage workers between 2022 and 2026 will require about $1.8 billion a year. Together with the enhanced Workfare, this will cost $9 billion over the next five years, compared with current expenditure on Workfare of around $850 million a year, excluding special payments.

The permanent GST Voucher Scheme will also be enhanced to provide continuing offsets for GST expenses for lower- to middle-income households, and most retiree households. However, the aim is not just to bolster social support via public spending, but also to encourage community giving. To this end, the Budget has included matching grants for charitable giving, as well as support for charities to build capabilities.

Social support must be complemented by social investment in order to sustain social mobility. Since the nation's independence, Singapore's social policy has been underpinned by substantial investment in education and housing. This was reaffirmed in this year's Budget, which announced the scaling-up of the KidSTART and UPLIFT programmes to give a further leg-up to children from lower-income households during their formative years.

REVIEWING GOVERNMENT SPENDING

Still, the "defining challenges of our time" identified in the Budget speech — including climate change and the rapidly ageing population — will generate fiscal pressures that cannot be addressed by higher taxes alone. This is why the Finance Minister alluded to fundamental changes to the healthcare system that will be needed to keep healthcare spending sustainable.

Recognising the scope to review the delivery of public services beyond healthcare, the announced additional 1 per cent cut to the budgets of Ministries and Organs of State from the next financial year will encourage discipline in public spending. By leveraging technology and behavioural insights, and reviewing organisation and processes, the public sector can raise efficiency in service delivery further still and contribute significantly towards keeping state finances on an even keel even as demands on the public purse expand.

The exhortation to "stand together" — to "keep faith with one another" — is the common thread that runs through Budget 2022. It underpins the continued investment in people, the effort to create opportunities for all, and adjustments to the tax system for greater equity.

While the Budget is an important statement of intent, much depends on whether citizens and stakeholders resonate with the values articulated. Do they agree Singapore must remain competitive and do what it takes to restructure the economy? Are companies prepared to pay higher wages, and the affluent higher taxes?

Ultimately, their response to the Budget will matter most.

Budget 2022 Sets the Pace for Singapore's Transformation

First published in The Straits Times on 23 February 2022

The need to be ready for the future is spoken of so often that it is easily taken for granted. Sometimes, it takes policy changes to focus minds and set things in motion. This is what Budget 2022 has accomplished. The suite of Budget measures, comprising new policy announcements as well as the fleshing out of previously announced policies, will force the pace of Singapore's economic and social transformation.

Revisions to taxes and manpower rules, in particular, will induce changes to business and household behaviour in line with Singapore's strategic priorities, notably the need for a competitive economy, greener future and more inclusive society.

Most of these policy moves were telegraphed well in advance of this year's budget. On the Goods and Services Tax (GST), it was only a question of when and how the hike would be implemented; as for the carbon tax, it was about the extent and pace of increase. Additional taxes on the wealthy were also anticipated, as were moves to increase the selectivity of foreign manpower.

Even so, Budget 2022 marks a decisive step forward for Singapore, taking the nation into the future with stronger public revenues and a renewed social compact. This was reflected not just in ambitious policy measures, but also an appeal to the values that infuse these policies with meaning.

In his Budget Statement, Minister for Finance Lawrence Wong spoke of the need to "stand together as one" and to "keep faith with one another", values that underpin the call to renew and strengthen the social compact.

AMBITIOUS BUT NOT UNREALISTIC

The Budget also signalled determination to transform Singapore's economy and society through policy measures that are ambitious but not unrealistic.

Underscoring Singapore's commitment to sustainability, the Government is bringing forward the timeline for the country to attain net zero carbon emissions. To achieve this, the carbon tax will be raised progressively to $50–$80 per tonne by 2030. This is higher than what some had anticipated, but well within the range of taxes already imposed by OECD economies, and with an eight-year runway to achieve.

Measures to keep foreign workforce growth sustainable have been stepped up since 2020. The latest revisions to Employment Pass (EP) and S Pass qualifying salaries are significant, the aim being to ensure that incoming EP and S pass holders are of comparable quality to the top one-third of the local workforce at corresponding skill levels. The Tier 1 S Pass levy will nearly double by 2025. The tighter dependency ratio ceilings for work permit holders in Construction and Process will also force companies in these sectors to raise productivity and reduce foreign manpower reliance.

It is worth considering what the various Budget policy measures amount to for businesses. Faced with a possible top-up to corporate tax, higher carbon and energy prices, as well as higher local and foreign manpower costs, it will not be business as usual. The aggregate impact of these measures will be unevenly felt across companies and sectors.

For firms, survival and success will depend on whether their business models are fit for the new normal, and if not, whether they can pivot to more sustainable ways of doing business. While the Government is providing significant transitional support to firms to offset the impact of the carbon price hike and progressive wages, support will taper over time. With timetables set for policy changes and transitional support, firms have a clear window in which to act.

Some firms will fold — whether forced to by changing market conditions, the ongoing pandemic or policy changes introduced in Budget 2022. This is to be expected in a dynamic economy where "creative destruction" is necessary to transform the economy and channel resources to the most productive uses.

Singapore must however continue to offer a strong value proposition for enterprises. A vibrant economy requires a critical mass of innovative firms that are able to leverage Singapore's infrastructure, trade networks, R&D base and skilled manpower to compete in global markets. Hence the emphasis in Budget 2022 on investment in the future: in digital capabilities, innovation, local enterprise and people. Only by remaining competitive can Singapore maintain relevance in the world and generate revenues to meet expanding social needs.

CARING WITHOUT CODDLING

While the market will weed out unviable firms, the calculus is different for citizens, with the intent for no one to be left behind. This year's Budget was a compassionate one that acknowledged the challenges of workers facing income loss or difficulty finding jobs, with extensions to both the COVID-19 Recovery Grant and Jobs Growth Incentive announced. The $560 million Household Support Package will help Singaporeans with utility bills, children's education and daily expenses. In view of rising prices, the GST hike will be implemented in two steps in 2023 and 2024, instead of taking effect this year. A further $640 million has been added to the $6 billion Assurance Package to cover at least five years of additional GST expenses for the majority of Singapore households.

On a permanent basis, Workfare payouts will be increased, and eligibility criteria broadened. Lower-wage workers also stand to gain from the expansion of the Progressive Wage Model. The permanent GST Voucher will be enhanced to provide continuing GST offsets to lower- to middle-income households and most retiree households.

Care and assurance, however, does not imply coddling. While citizens will have their needs well provided for, they are also expected to take responsibility for themselves and their families. There remains a strong impetus to reskill and improve oneself, with the Government providing funding to the National Trades Union Congress (NTUC) to scale up Company Training Committees, and making company attachments for mature mid-career workers a permanent feature of the training and placement ecosystem. Social investment — whether in public housing or education — remains the principal means by which the state helps citizens to build better lives for themselves.

Much as Budget 2022 was inclusive, it did not fully address every area of need or every segment of society. An advisory committee is still working on measures to help online platform workers, while the Enabling Masterplan 2030 will provide further support for persons with disabilities when it is launched later this year. Plans to support caregivers and boost mental health are also forthcoming. While the Government is studying the recommendations of the joint NTUC and Singapore National Employers Federation taskforce on professionals, managers and executives (PMEs), details of measures such as supplementary unemployment income relief have yet to be announced.

REIMAGINING SOCIAL SUPPORT

Budget 2022 builds on existing pillars of social support, which have been strengthened through successive budgets, accompanied by higher tax contributions from the better-off. Where does this stop, some wonder. Will social support be continually expanded, and will the wealthy have to shoulder an ever-increasing burden?

Fiscal systems perform the necessary role of redistribution, but the concept of redistribution itself is transactional. In families and close-knit communities, we speak instead of mutual support and obligation, whether mediated through the state or directly among members.

Looking ahead, there may be merit in positioning social transfers not just as support for the less well-off, but as a benefit of citizenship — with the aim of providing assurance for all and sharing the fruits of progress equitably. Now that Workfare has been extended to over half a million workers and the GST Voucher to middle-income households, support is no long "residual" or targeted at just a small minority who are unable to get by on their own. If such support continues to be extended to more citizens and households, it will not be too far a step to recast social support schemes as a "social dividend" — benefitting all citizens but tiered according to means for better targeting and fiscal sustainability.

As Singaporeans, we celebrate success together and support one another through difficult times. This sense of solidarity, so important for a nation, is difficult to sustain when there are wide gaps in pay across occupations, and when those from different socio-economic strata lead vastly different lives.

Budget 2022 — in moving changes to Workfare, social support and taxes, and encouraging charitable giving — weaves the themes of inclusiveness and solidarity, of "(having) each other's back". It sets out a clear vision — founded on values, and fleshed out in specific measures and timelines — for Singapore's progress as a society and nation.

Many Lines of Defence Are Needed to Keep Inflation at Bay

First published in The Straits Times on 2 June 2022

Amid rising inflation due to war, pandemic and supply chain snarls, governments across the world have to find ways and means of keeping the cost of living manageable for their citizens. For Singapore, too, this is arguably the most pressing near-term challenge.

Helping businesses and citizens cope with rising costs requires a multipronged approach, using various policy levers in tandem, while individuals and the community must also do their part.

STRONG DOLLAR, CASH TRANSFERS

The first line of defence against rising prices is monetary policy — maintaining a strong Singapore dollar to keep the lid on imported inflation. Next are cash transfers and subsidies to help citizens and households with the costs of essentials, including food, utilities and public services. Besides permanent subsidies for healthcare, housing and other public amenities, citizens have received one-off income tax rebates and cash transfers.

Since 2021, two tranches of Community Development Council (CDC) vouchers have been distributed to all Singaporean households to help with the cost of living, besides the initial aim of thanking Singaporeans for their solidarity during COVID-19. This mode of assistance may appear odd, since consumers would enjoy greater flexibility from direct cash transfers of equivalent value.

In fact, CDC vouchers are like a cash handout as they can be used for hawker food as well as goods and services at heartland stores — items which the vast majority of Singaporeans would have purchased anyway. This is in contrast to the SingapoRediscovers Vouchers, which were meant to stimulate domestic tourism demand to offset the fall in visitor arrivals during the COVID-19 pandemic. The decision to allow the 2023 and 2024 CDC vouchers to be spent at major supermarket chains will make them practically equivalent to cash.

Some have commented that this would erode the benefit to heartland stores ("Hawkers, small retailers will lose out once CDC vouchers can be used at supermarkets", *The Straits Times* forum letter, May 18). However, the vouchers' impact on aggregate demand for heartland stores probably has been modest compared to their role in shifting existing demand towards vendors in the scheme. The primary objective of the vouchers should be to help citizens with the cost of living, with any benefit to heartland stores an added bonus.

Besides CDC vouchers, the $560 million Budget 2022 Household Support Package includes additional utilities rebates and top-ups to child development and education accounts. This array of measures is aimed at blunting the sharp edge of inflation for consumers. Singapore's core inflation, which excludes the cost of private transport and accommodation, hit 3.3 per cent in April this year, the highest in over a decade. With global fuel and commodity prices surging, the Monetary Authority of Singapore projects that core inflation could peak at 4 per cent, and headline inflation at 5–6 per cent, later this year.

PUBLIC POLICY — FOCUS ON AFFORDABILITY

A third line of defence against cost of living pressures may be less obvious but just as important — efforts to manage supply and demand, the impact of which is more likely to be felt over the medium to longer term. While Singapore is a price taker for many global commodities, there is much the

Government can do to influence the supply and demand of goods and services, and hence costs.

For instance, a steady, adequate supply of residential and commercial land helps to keep housing prices and commercial rents stable even as demand flows and ebbs. Diversification of imported food sources over time has increased Singapore's resilience to supply-induced price shocks in specific markets. It is also important to promote market competition and protect consumers against anti-competitive business practices. The provision of amenities and services by public agencies has a direct bearing on the cost of living, with efficient public management translating into lower costs for consumers.

On the demand side, reforms to healthcare insurance — including a minimum co-payment of 5 per cent for Integrated Shield plans — will help to manage healthcare consumption, and hence healthcare inflation. Additional buyer stamp duties are among the "macroprudential" policy measures adopted by the Monetary Authority of Singapore to rein in surging housing prices. Encouraging hybrid workplaces, including the flexibility to work from home, may also help workers save on commuting costs at a time of elevated fuel prices.

Going a step further, affordability should be elevated to a key objective in public policy and service delivery, with a deliberate effort to provide Singaporeans with low-cost options. Take food, for example. Hawker centres have been instrumental in keeping cooked food affordable in Singapore. A decision was taken in 2011 to resume building hawker centres after a 26-year hiatus. Subletting of hawker stalls, which had driven up rents, was disallowed in 2012, while the minimum reserve rent was also abolished.

However, commercially operated coffeeshops and food courts account for a significant share of the market. Last month, it was reported that over half of stallholders in a Toa Payoh coffeeshop decided not to renew their leases after the new management had doubled the rent. With imported food prices climbing, rental hikes will only exacerbate the cost pressures on cooked-food stallholders. What could help going forward is to expand and improve the social enterprise model for hawker centres and food courts.

In public housing, there has been increasing demand for larger flats as Singaporeans become more affluent. Still, having a good mix of flat types, including two- and three-room units, is important to give families more options in keeping with their financial circumstances.

With public amenities and services, service-level decisions can affect affordability without compromising the principle of cost recovery. While service providers are not wrong to focus on customer experience, not all public services have to be premium services if these translate into higher costs for the public. For instance, non-air conditioned hospital wards, classrooms and public buses can help to save on energy costs, besides being more environmentally friendly. Some degree of creature comfort may be necessary to encourage commuters to choose public transport over cars and taxis, but options such as cycling and walking could also gain popularity if made more convenient and comfortable.

Affordable leisure options are important for Singapore to be an inclusive home. Public parks, beaches and playgrounds are free recreational spaces that can be enjoyed by all, while citizens have access to public museums and sports facilities at zero or nominal cost.

At the same time, these common spaces ought to be paired with affordable dining options. When the National Parks Board leases out premises for food operators, for example, it seeks a balance between revenue maximisation and the provision of affordable food options to the public.

In taking various planning decisions, government agencies should keep a laser focus on affordability, particularly at a time when inflation is rising. Design thinking — often used to improve customer experience — may be a useful tool, by focusing on the daily needs and experiences of lower-income citizens. This could entail mapping out a citizen's journey in performing daily tasks, and identifying suitable policy levers to ease costs and expand options.

CITIZENS MUST PLAY THEIR PART

While the Government has a key role to play in managing the cost of living, there is much, too, that citizens can do to optimise their spending and finances. The first step is financial planning — to insure against medical and other contingencies, to avoid becoming financially overextended and to set aside enough for long-term expenditure priorities. Exercising prudence in spending, looking out for lower-cost alternatives, conserving utilities, and sharing resources within families and communities, are among the many ways in which household budgets can be stretched.

On the revenue ledger, Singaporeans can seek ways to augment employment income with passive income streams and renew their skills for better earnings prospects. Finally, communities can step up to lend a helping hand to those in need. Whether small business owners, social enterprises, volunteer groups, or community and religious organisations, all can play their part in helping the vulnerable to cope with financial stress. This will have the added benefit of building solidarity and strengthening bonds within society.

Call the Sports Hub Public-Private Partnership a Failure or Not, That is Not the Point

First published by CNA on 17 June 2022

The early termination of the Sports Hub public-private partnership (PPP) has sparked renewed discussion on whether such partnerships are suitable for providing public services with social aims.

National agency Sport Singapore (SportSG) announced on Jun 10 that it would be taking over the ownership and management of the Singapore Sports Hub from Dec 9. This will terminate the PPP with private sector consortium SportsHub Pte Ltd (SHPL), which had been planned to run from 2010 to 2035.

Yet, SportSG CEO Lim Teck Yin said that it was not correct to conclude that the PPP had failed, on the basis that the right to terminate had been built into the agreement and that the evolving context made it "the right time to do this".

However one wishes to characterise the Sports Hub PPP, it is clear that innovation, so important for progress, does not always work out. What is key is to learn quickly from experience and pivot to more effective ways to meet public needs. It is also important not to tar all PPPs with the same brush, but to understand the specific conditions that make it more likely or not for a PPP to succeed.

WHY A PUBLIC-PRIVATE PARTNERSHIP WAS SOUGHT FOR THE SPORTS HUB

Singapore's principal motivation for PPPs has been to tap on private sector expertise for innovation and efficiency in projects that the public sector pays to use. Since their systematic introduction in the United Kingdom in the 1990s, PPPs have gained traction in many countries for projects spanning transport, utilities, schools, hospitals and even prisons.

Beginning in the early 2000s, Singapore pursued PPPs to develop desalination, NEWater and incineration plants, as well as social infrastructure, notably the Institute of Technical Education (ITE) College West and the Singapore Sports Hub.

For example, Singapore's Jurong Island desalination plant, officially opened in April, leverages the strengths of a private consortium formed by two companies — ST Engineering provided expertise and design innovation for greater energy efficiency, while the plant derives synergies from co-location with Tuas Power's power plant.

For the Sports Hub, it was thought that private-sector networks would be key to unlocking value by bringing in major sporting and entertainment events, to maximise utilisation of the facility. Of course, one possible model was for the Government to build the Sports Hub and then engage event management companies to run the programming.

But that would not have allowed for upstream involvement of stakeholders to share the risks and optimise the design to make it fit for their purposes. Sharing project risks between the public and private sectors is often seen as instilling financial discipline as the private operator has an incentive to ensure the financial viability of the project.

This was a highly ambitious project. As the world's largest integrated sports infrastructure PPP project, it stood in contrast to the many cookie-cutter building projects typically put through PPP in other countries. Besides the significant capital needed and complex build requirements, the project involved service providers spanning different business sectors, such as retail, catering and commercial rights, making this a particularly complex undertaking.

DID SOCIAL AND COMMERCIAL OBJECTIVES DIVERGE TOO GREATLY?

The PPP appeared to have paid off in some ways, as the Sports Hub succeeded in bringing in high-profile events such as the Women's Tennis Association finals, making Singapore the first city in the Asia-Pacific to host the prestigious tournament. Other prominent events held at the Sports Hub included the HSBC World Rugby Sevens series and concerts by global superstars like Madonna, Coldplay, Jay Chou and BTS.

But the main sticking point seems to have been the availability of the facility for local and community sporting events. In announcing the takeover, SportSG said the move would give it greater control and flexibility, and there are plans to make it more accessible to the broader community for sports and other social uses.

The natural question is whether SportSG's vision could have been achieved under the PPP. SportSG's Mr Lim referred to "contractual limitations" that stood in the way of unlocking the full value of the Sports Hub for the community. Here is where the commercial objectives of the private consortium may be in tension with the public objective of promoting a sporting culture in Singapore. As former Sports Hub CEO Oon Jin Teik commented, it has been challenging to find the balance between profit making and providing a public service.

CAN THE PPP MODEL WORK FOR PUBLIC SERVICES?

Profit making is not incompatible with public service delivery if the incentives for the private operator are aligned with public aims, whether this is achieved through the revenue model or regulatory supervision. For PPPs, incentive alignment is all the more important given the long tenure of contracts and the need to respond flexibly to end-user needs.

A PPP may be likened to a marriage, given the long-term nature of the contract. It needs mutual understanding, good communication and a spirit of give-and-take. Not everything can be spelt out in a contract nor can every eventuality be foreseen, so flexibility should be built in where possible.

What is clear from Singapore's experience is that some factors make it more likely or otherwise for a PPP to succeed. In the case of the NEWater plants, private sector capabilities and business synergies helped to achieve cost efficiency. Where output is standardised and easily monitored, and the underlying technology is stable, PPP contracts are better able to regulate private service providers and ensure that public needs are well catered for over the long haul.

In contrast, changing technology and end-user needs require frequent renegotiation between the public agency and private sector partner, which may prove challenging even with the best of intents. Cases like the Sports Hub suggest that PPPs may be less well-suited for social infrastructure where commercial and social objectives diverge, and where even contractual flexibility may not be able to meet ever-changing user needs. It is noteworthy that following the development of ITE College West through PPP, ITE chose to develop College Central via traditional procurement instead.

Looking back, the scale and complexity of the Sports Hub project suggested that it was always going to be an uphill climb to balance the needs of all stakeholders. The parting of ways between SportSG and SHPL will give the Sports Hub the opportunity to reset and refocus on its core social mission.

This is one of several instances where the public sector has changed course decisively upon assessment of the situation and outlook. In this way, implementation informs public policy even as policy directs implementation.

Addressing Inflation While Staying the Course on Medium-Term Priorities

First published by CNA on 2 August 2022 with the title "Fighting inflation is more than having higher wages offset cost of living increases"

Singapore's core inflation continues ticking upwards. Official data released on Jul 25 showed a 4.4 per cent year-on-year increase in June, the highest since November 2008 amid the Global Financial Crisis.

Although the Monetary Authority of Singapore (MAS) has projected it to ease after peaking in the third quarter, core inflation is expected to remain high at around 3.5 per cent to 4 per cent towards the end of the year. This is unsurprising given continued global supply chain disruptions, the ongoing Russia-Ukraine war and the lasting effects of the COVID-19 pandemic, from which Singapore is unable to fully insulate itself.

Rising prices will affect all Singaporeans, particularly the lower- to middle-income, who spend a large part of their budget on essential items like food and utilities.

IS A WAGE-PRICE SPIRAL LIKELY?

Faced with a higher cost of living, will workers demand larger pay raises? Some are worried that a wage-price spiral could be in the making. This is when workers ask for higher wages to offset inflation and maintain purchasing power, and employers in turn raise prices to offset higher labour costs. When inflationary expectations become entrenched, it becomes difficult for regulators to bring down inflation without incurring the high costs of slower growth and higher unemployment.

However, there are reasons to believe a wage-price spiral may not take root here. MAS Managing Director Ravi Menon pointed out in July that automatic wage indexation is not common in Singapore, and that the pass-through from prices to wages has been historically weak. This is in contrast to countries like Belgium and Luxembourg, where salaries are automatically adjusted according to inflation, a practice that may be difficult to sustain as prices soar.

For a wage-price spiral to occur, higher wages also need to be passed on to consumers through higher prices. The extent to which this happens varies by sector depending on the share of labour cost in total business cost, as well as the strength of market demand for different goods and services. Higher productivity can also help offset increased labour costs.

Notwithstanding, there remain risks if wage growth outstrips productivity growth over a sustained period. The labour market in Singapore is tight and is expected to remain so for some time. In the first quarter of 2022, the ratio of job vacancies to unemployed people was at its highest since 1998, suggesting that it has not been easy to fill vacancies with locals, while the size of the non-resident workforce remains below its pre-COVID level.

NAVIGATING POLICY TIGHTROPES

All these point to several policy tightropes which the Government has to navigate in the ensuing months.

The first is how quickly and forcefully to tighten monetary policy. The MAS recently announced its fourth policy tightening move since October 2021. The Singapore dollar has appreciated, even hitting record levels against major currencies including the yen, the euro and the British pound.

The appreciation in the Singapore dollar against most major trading partners has helped to stem imported inflation and eased price pressures by crimping aggregate demand, but this will come at the cost of slower economic growth.

This is a balance policymakers elsewhere are grappling with too. The United States Federal Reserve has been attempting a "soft landing", raising interest rates to bring prices under control while trying not to tip the economy into recession. The MAS can likewise be expected to take a calibrated approach, balancing the need for price stability and economic growth.

A second question is whether to go ahead with the Goods and Services Tax (GST) increase of 1 percentage point in 2023 and another percentage point in 2024, and whether to defer carbon tax hikes planned between 2024 and 2030. This is about whether medium-term imperatives — for sound public finances and the green transition — should be put on hold while Singapore grapples with rising prices.

But since inflation may stay elevated for some time, there is not necessarily a better window in which to raise GST, and structural spending needs continue to grow. As for the carbon tax, there is still time for businesses to make the necessary adjustments before the planned tax increases from 2024 onwards.

STAYING THE COURSE ON LABOUR MARKET ADJUSTMENT

Given the hard realities of containing inflation, the question becomes one of helping citizens and households tide over this storm. Fortunately, Singapore has the means to provide relief in the form of a S$1.5 billion support package announced in June.

Help will remain targeted at the lower-income and more vulnerable, as a broad fiscal stimulus risks further stoking inflation. Deputy Prime Minister and Finance Minister Lawrence Wong has indicated that the Government will continue to monitor the economic situation and could provide further support if necessary.

Relief packages, however, cannot be sustained indefinitely if inflation remains elevated into next year and beyond. It will be necessary to find structural solutions — whether larger permanent transfers, higher wages underpinned by higher productivity, or a combination of these.

The pace of labour market adjustments also has to be considered in the light of immediate cost pressures. A key initiative is the Progressive

Wage Model, which aims to raise the pay of lower-wage workers across various sectors and occupations, in tandem with skills upgrading and increased productivity. This will help to shape a more inclusive society where all workers are valued and paid fairly for their contributions.

Another set of policy moves is intended to calibrate the inflow of foreign workers. These include raising the minimum salary requirements for Employment and S Pass holders, raising S Pass levies and tightening the Dependency Ratio Ceilings in the Construction and Process sectors.

These initiatives, while critical for a sustainable and resilient workforce, contribute to higher wage and business costs. It would however be unwise to backtrack on structural adjustments that have longer-term policy objectives when we still have other ways to manage the impact of inflation.

Instead, effort could be directed at improving the efficiency of labour market matching while facilitating the entry of foreign workers to plug critical gaps in the workforce. The impact of higher labour costs could also be mitigated by redoubling efforts at raising automation and productivity, and through upskilling and reskilling workers.

Still, it would be best to defer for now any further policy moves, beyond what has been announced, that may exacerbate the labour supply crunch and push up wages and prices further.

Finding the right policy balance will be necessary to steer the economy through the inflationary tempest while keeping our sights trained on the goal of a competitive, future-oriented, inclusive and sustainable Singapore.

Part C
Politics and Society

Making Democracy Work

First published in The Straits Times on 26 October 2021

A Pew Research Centre survey of nearly 19,000 people in 17 advanced economies this year found considerable public dissatisfaction with how democracy is working in many of these economies. Fewer than half of respondents in Greece, Italy, Spain, Japan, the United States, France and Belgium indicated satisfaction with their democracy. By contrast, over three-quarters of respondents in Singapore, Sweden and New Zealand were satisfied with the political system, according to the Pew findings published last week (Oct 21).

While democracies across the world vary considerably in form and practice, some today see democracy itself in crisis, facing challenges from within and without. Globally, populism and entrenched partisanship have had wide-ranging ramifications, from Brexit to distrust of vaccines. The proliferation of "fake news" is undermining the very foundations of a political system that depends on the informed choices of citizens. Democratic states have also been the target of election meddling and hostile information campaigns orchestrated from abroad.

The principal threat to democracy from within is the prioritisation of partisan interests above all. Too often, political parties focus on tearing down competing ideas and proposals, rather than drawing on the rich reservoir of ideas for policy solutions. Challengers may seek the downfall of the incumbent even at the expense of the national good. For instance, the clash between Democrats and Republicans over the United States debt ceiling has pushed the government to the brink of default. When political polarisation sets in, it can poison relationships in the community, workplace and even within families.

A question worth pondering is: can a democratic system be envisaged that promotes constructive democratic discourse by rewarding both the ruling and opposition political parties for successful policy outcomes?

Some may dismiss this out of hand. After all, politics in a democracy is a contest, with winners and losers. More often than not, a zero-sum contest will turn ugly. This need not, however, deter the idealist from envisioning a political system where the competition of ideas builds up rather than tears down society.

If there is truth in Winston Churchill's observation that "democracy is the worst form of government, except all those other forms that have been tried", then it behoves those of a democratic persuasion to try to make democracy work better. Success is more likely when the main political parties are centrist, and not so far apart ideologically that they are unable to engage in constructive discourse. This opens up the possibility of cross-fertilising ideas to tackle policy challenges.

REFRAMING THE CONTEST OF IDEAS

For competing ideas to work to a country's advantage, those in power should be able to co-opt the best ideas, including those put forward by opposition parties, without being perceived to cave in to pressure or otherwise lose political points.

How can this be achieved?

First, governments should look ahead and take pre-emptive measures to tackle public grievances and emerging societal fault lines before they become political crises. In Singapore, such issues include the socio-economic divide, and discrimination on the basis of race or nationality, which were addressed at the National Day Rally this year.

Timely intervention could save governments from being seen to buckle under public pressure when inaction finally becomes untenable, which would invite greater pressure on other issues in the future. Any reform is best made from a position of strength rather than weakness. This requires those in power to have their ear close to the ground, and their finger on the pulse of the nation.

Second, government leaders should try to avoid taking a dogmatic stance on issues from which it would be hard to walk back later. These could include specific forms of social support or how the public purse ought to be used. Ironclad pronouncements on such issues only constrain the policy space. It would be better to explain to the public why a particular policy is adopted or otherwise, but leave open the possibility for change should it become warranted.

Fringe voices — those whose views are far from the mainstream — are often dismissed as naïve or misguided, but the arc of history suggests that today's heterodoxy may well become tomorrow's orthodoxy. There needs to be a safe space for contrarian ideas to be debated — otherwise, only the most strident dissenters will be heard.

Third, those who have been early cheerleaders should resist the urge to claim sole credit for an idea that is eventually implemented, or to contend that they had forced the government's hand. In Singapore, universal healthcare insurance, enhanced healthcare benefits for the older generation, as well as wage floors for lower-wage workers, were all ideas in circulation long before MediShield Life, the Pioneer Generation Package or the Progressive Wage Model (in its latest incarnation) were introduced.

In truth, a successful policy often has many "parents" — political parties, civic organisations, academics and citizens — whose advocacy and input over the years have made a difference. Sometimes, it may take time for policies to move into the zone of broad acceptability as circumstances change and public attitudes evolve. It follows that those in government need not be shy about adopting ideas and policies advanced by political rivals or civil society groups. On its part, the administration ought to be generous in acknowledging stakeholders' contribution to policy development.

In functioning democracies, policies typically go through a period of contestation and gestation, with stakeholders pitching in views that help to shape policy and refine it, even after implementation. Recognising contributions and validating differences in view can go a long way in encouraging constructive participation, rather than destructive division, in the policy formation process.

WHAT'S THE ALTERNATIVE?

For some, autocratic systems like China offer a compelling alternative to liberal democracy. Free from the strictures of democratic contestation, the Chinese government has been able to execute social and economic reforms in ways that would be unthinkable in the West: banning for-profit tuition, limiting the time children can spend on video games and curbing the monopolistic practices of its Internet giants. It may be argued that these policies benefit society, and have been carried out at a speed that would be impossible in a system with greater restraints on the executive.

The comparative vulnerabilities of liberal democracies and autocracies are evident in their very different approaches towards information control, and the consequent challenges they face. If democracies are plagued by a surfeit of questionable news and misinformation, authoritarian regimes suffer as much or more from a deficit of independent, trusted information. Where the overriding priority is to stamp out any challenge to authority, alternative voices are muzzled, and accountability and transparency given short shrift. Inordinately constricting the flow of ideas and information also hampers intellectual dynamism and innovation over the long run.

By contrast, the dilemma facing democracies is how to prevent misinformation and hostile foreign interference from poisoning democratic discourse, while not giving the state carte blanche to quash dissenting views. This is at the heart of the recent debates in Singapore over the Protection from Online Falsehoods and Manipulation Act (POFMA) and the Foreign Interference (Countermeasures) Act (FICA).

US President Joe Biden has described democracies and autocracies as being locked in a struggle for ideological dominance. In his first address to Congress in April, he contended that "the autocrats of the world" were betting that America's democracy would fail. It was up to the US, he said, to "prove democracy still works". As he observed in an interview, the challenge facing democracies is whether they can arrive at consensus within a timeframe that would allow them to compete with autocracies.

REIMAGINING DEMOCRACY

Still, democracy possesses considerable advantages, not least the system of checks and balances against the unbridled exercise of state power. There is also tremendous potential value in the contest of ideas, which can help democracies identify policy blind spots more easily than autocracies, benevolent or otherwise.

A democracy that derives strength from this would require responsible political parties and a discerning electorate that rewards constructive politics through the ballot box — and potentially in other ways limited only by the imagination.

Rather than adopting the posture of gladiators in a fight to the death, the ruling and opposition parties should see themselves as two sides belonging to the same team, their sparring on the training field helping to hone instincts and make the team itself more competitive.

This, of course, requires the parties to play ball, on a level playing field; it requires stakeholders to shed an "us versus them" mindset and seek unity in diversity. Once political polarisation becomes entrenched, however, the window of opportunity to achieve this would have closed, perhaps irrevocably.

Political systems must be well-adapted to each country's unique history, culture, demographics and society. However, a constructive, competitive democracy is a worthwhile aspiration — whether in South-east Asia, Europe or any other part of the world.

A Year of Obstinate Hope

First published in The Straits Times on 22 December 2021

The year 2021 has been one in which our capacity for hope has been well and truly tested. Many Singaporeans have experienced stress, anxiety and burnout — whether from work or caregiving demands, social isolation or safe management measures arising from the pandemic. Families have lost loved ones to COVID-19, while familiar establishments such as Bugis Food Junction and Chinatown Food Street have shut for good.

Over the year, our capacity for hope was continually tested. Hope was kindled each time COVID-19 restrictions were relaxed, only to be dashed later by a tightening up as COVID infections rose. For many of us, it has been hard to shrug off the feeling that we have been going around in circles, driven by the caprices of the evolving pandemic.

Yet, as we look back on 2021, it is worth recognising how far we have come — in terms of living with the virus, as well as in building a more resilient, inclusive and sustainable future. As we hope, again, for a better year ahead, it is worth remembering that we do have agency in how we respond to challenges, and that we never walk alone.

DASHED, REKINDLED, RINSE, REPEAT

Entering 2021, there was reason to be hopeful that COVID-19 would finally be tamed. Vaccines had been developed with unprecedented speed and were being rolled out worldwide. By the middle of the year, however, the emergence of the delta variant put paid to any notion of a quick end to the pandemic. The goalposts were ever-shifting. Initially, it was said that herd immunity would be attained with 60–70 per cent of the population vaccinated; later, experts raised this to over 90 per cent.

For much of the year, Singapore succeeded in keeping the virus at bay, although there were occasional outbreaks such as those linked to imported cases, KTV joints and the Jurong Fishery Port. Then in September, daily infections and deaths began to mount despite an aggressive vaccination drive. This left many Singaporeans with a feeling of helplessness — progress in vaccination slowed as the rate topped 80 per cent, and it was unclear what more could be done.

In dealing with the public health crisis, Singapore's approach recognised the economic need to gradually open up for business, while avoiding the high human toll that would come with throwing off the shackles of safe management measures entirely. Attempts to tailor policy to the prevailing health situation resulted in ever-changing regulations, with the limit on public gatherings toggling between two and five persons. This fuelled an emotional roller-coaster ride for many Singaporeans, particularly those working in affected sectors such as hospitality and F&B.

Still, there is no mistaking the government's commitment to steer the country towards endemic COVID while aiming for a soft landing. Vaccinated travel lanes have rapidly opened up, and Singapore has begun to host international conferences again. Unemployment has trended down, while daily COVID infections are finally on the wane.

The appearance of the omicron variant in November has thrown yet another spanner in the works for a COVID-weary nation and world. We can take solace in the knowledge that booster shots offer some protection against it, while new antiviral drugs could reduce the risk of severe illness. Meanwhile, pharmaceutical companies are racing to develop vaccines targeted at the new variant.

A MORE RESILIENT FUTURE

Omicron will not, in any case, be the last threat to public health. As humanity prepares for the future "Disease X", we can consider the current pandemic a necessary wake-up call, underscoring the importance of resilience in public healthcare systems, vaccine readiness and supply chains across the globe.

In Singapore, COVID-19 has been a catalyst to improve living conditions for migrant workers; it has also raised public awareness of the crucial role played by healthcare and frontline service workers. Resilience and equity are taking their place alongside efficiency as key priorities guiding public policy and business decisions.

A MORE INCLUSIVE, COHESIVE SOCIETY

While the pandemic has disrupted life in many ways, Singapore cannot put the future on hold. The year has seen Singapore take significant steps forward in tackling medium-term challenges.

Notably, efforts have been made to acknowledge and address societal divides, such as those of race, religion, nationality and income. Policy measures announced at the National Day Rally in August included a significant expansion of the Progressive Wage Model to support many more lower-wage workers, legislation to address discrimination in the job market and approval for female Muslim nurses to wear the tudung while in uniform.

Beyond policy and legislation, building a more inclusive and cohesive society requires open and honest conversations among Singaporeans in a spirit of mutual respect and understanding. There is hope as long as a critical mass of fair-minded Singaporeans is able to find common ground, despite their differences, so that ideological polarisation does not take root here.

A STABLE AND SUSTAINABLE WORLD

On the international front, 2021 began with some observers expressing hope that the change in the US administration would precipitate a thaw in US-China relations. Many also hoped that COP-26 would see a revitalisation of global efforts to combat climate change. On both issues, the best-case scenario failed to materialise, but we can at least be thankful that the worst case did not come to pass either.

Singapore, as a small state, has again had to find ways to ride the waves from shifting geopolitical tides. As tensions between the G2 rivals ratcheted up, Singapore played host to US Vice-President Kamala Harris in August and Chinese Foreign Minister Wang Yi in September.

In the fight against climate change, Singapore is stepping up to the plate as a responsible global citizen, recognising that sustainability is in our enlightened self-interest. Climate mitigation will affect companies and households here in many ways in the coming years — from the transformation of Jurong Island into a sustainable energy and chemicals park, to supermarkets charging customers for plastic bags.

THE YEAR AHEAD

Several issues are already on our minds: Will omicron and other COVID-19 variants continue to hold us in thrall, or will Singapore and the world finally be able to treat the disease as endemic? Will persistent inflation force a tightening of global monetary conditions, or will central banks keep interest rates low? Will the US and China feel their way towards a new modus vivendi, or will rivalry intensify, dividing the world into competing spheres of influence? Domestically, will the 4G political leaders settle on a first among equals? When will GST be raised, and will there be new wealth taxes?

Confronted with known and unknown "unknowns", we as human beings are nonetheless wired to cling to hope amid adversity. Some of us place our trust in the divine, others in human ingenuity and resolve. We may find hope in the everyday heroism of frontline healthcare workers, or in the achievements of sporting heroes such as national shuttler Loh Kean Yew, who overcame a string of higher-ranked opponents en route to becoming badminton world champion.

What may also help is to recognise that we all retain agency, despite the curveballs lobbed in our direction by a mutating virus. For instance, we can take sensible steps to protect ourselves and loved ones from the virus without becoming hermits — by getting our vaccine shots, observing personal hygiene and adhering to safe management measures. We can even find purpose in helping to combat misinformation, or reaching out to those in distress with a listening ear and a helping hand.

We may take advantage of lifestyle changes forced on us by the pandemic to discard poor habits and limiting mindsets, and to embrace more sustainable ways of living and working. Just as small states may retain agency in navigating geopolitical shifts, individuals can likewise exercise agency in how we respond to the challenges in our homes, workplaces and society.

It is also important to remember that we are not alone. There are others who share our struggles, and those we can lean on for support within our communities or the larger Singapore family. Sometimes, all it takes is to ask for help. By joining hands with others in society, we can also make greater headway against the scourges of disease, disunity and environmental degradation than we can by ourselves.

We are leaving behind a year of ups and downs, some of us bone-weary, others recharged and ready to go. The new year beckons, with promise and uncertainty in equal measure — but also with hope rooted in personal agency, purpose and collective action.

In a Storm-Tossed World, Who's Going to Steer Your Ship?

First published in The Straits Times on 7 January 2022

Imagine yourself on a storm-tossed ship, trying to navigate treacherous waters with limited visibility. Who would you prefer at the helm? A steady consensus-builder like former German chancellor Angela Merkel, or a charismatic but chaotic leader like British Prime Minister Boris Johnson? Or perhaps someone single-minded and ruthless, like Russian President Vladimir Putin?

The question of leadership is as old as human civilisation. It is in focus particularly during leadership transitions, where much hangs on the vision, values and policies of those taking over. The past year saw many such transitions, with new heads of government installed in the United States, Germany, Japan and Malaysia. In the corporate world, the founders of Amazon and Twitter stepped aside for new blood. Leadership also changed hands at several major Singapore companies, including Singtel, StarHub, OCBC Bank and Temasek.

Over the years, many have attempted to distil the essence of good leadership. There is the "Great Man" leadership theory — that those born with certain traits are destined for greatness. This has, however, lost ground to theories of contingent leadership that emphasise the need for different leadership traits in different contexts. The UK's wartime leader Winston Churchill, for instance, is credited with rallying the nation in its bleakest hour, but fared less well as a peacetime prime minister.

The political and economic upheavals in recent years — exacerbated by COVID-19 — have focused minds on what it takes to lead in conditions that are volatile, uncertain, complex and ambiguous (VUCA).

LEADERSHIP OR LUCK?

Where risks and opportunities abound, a single misstep could undo decades of good work, while a judicious move could see fortunes swiftly made. Is success, then, a matter of leadership or luck? What leadership traits, if any, are needed to take a successful country or organisation forward?

The impact of leadership is often evident in squandered resources, loss of trust and damaged morale under venal or incompetent leaders — or conversely, new initiatives, solidarity and growth under capable and committed leaders.

Behind the rise and fall of empires and institutions are also structural forces such as demography, technology, geopolitics and societal change. While it is the task of leaders to respond to such changes, the future is difficult to predict — the best-laid plans may be thwarted by tectonic shifts in the operating environment. Time and chance also matter. "I would rather have a general who was lucky than one who was good," Napoleon Bonaparte is said to have remarked.

Overattributing outcomes to leadership may in fact skew decision-making. Consider the frequent turnover of team managers in elite football — sometimes, just a bad run of results can see a manager sacked, never mind the fine margins in games which can turn on borderline refereeing decisions. All too often, a manager who is dismissed from a team goes on to achieve success with another.

The award of large performance-linked bonuses to chief executive officers and fund managers may have also led to prioritising short-term financial results over sustainable growth. For critics of executive pay, the Global Financial Crisis in 2008–2009 added grist to the mill — losses were socialised when companies had to be bailed out by taxpayers, in stark contrast to the privatisation of gains in years of good growth.

THE MANAGEMENT OF SUCCESS

There is no denying the difference that good leadership can make in business and government. Credit must go to Singapore's first generation of political leaders for the remarkable economic and social transformation in the 1960s and 1970s. The pioneer leadership's judgment was not always right, but Singapore can count itself fortunate they were right more often than not, especially on the issues that mattered most. Subsequent generations of leaders built on this success, taking Singapore further and sometimes in new directions.

The demands on leadership will continually evolve as organisations mature. A company or country in the start-up phase needs to build up systems and processes, mobilise resources and win the confidence of stakeholders.

The management of success is a different task — leaders have to consider when to keep to strategies that brought success, and when to pivot to new approaches as circumstances change. This may entail making calculated bets to set the firm or the nation on a new arc of progress. Any change in approach will invariably create winners and losers, and is likely to run up against vested interests. Success in this endeavour requires strategic vision, powers of persuasion and effective implementation — traits long associated with good leadership.

In an age of pluralism and social media, leaders are also expected to cut an empathetic figure with a broad appeal. Two further ingredients are key in VUCA conditions: leaders would do well to harness collective wisdom, and to heed the unseen but essential.

HARNESSING COLLECTIVE WISDOM

No one has a monopoly of wisdom or expertise. The complexity of large organisations today means those at the top are unlikely to have an in-depth understanding of every area of operations, even if they have been through tours of duty in different departments. So it is important for leaders to consult widely.

Much attention has rightly been devoted to improving diversity within organisations and management teams, but these efforts will achieve little in an environment that fosters groupthink. Leaders who shut down staff at meetings, or who selectively listen to a favoured few, will have less opportunity to have their viewpoints challenged or their perspectives broadened. By contrast, those who create safe spaces for people to speak up can harness diverse perspectives to address complex and ambiguous challenges.

This is not to suggest that leaders should not hold firm convictions, or that they must be swayed by every opinion that is advanced. However, listening with an open mind allows leaders to unlock insights and experience within an organisation that can inform both planning and execution.

HEEDING THE UNSEEN BUT ESSENTIAL

Leaders in the private sector are typically assessed by financial performance or concrete indicators such as customer acquisition. In the public or non-profit sector, recognition may be given for new services, programmes or initiatives. Success, however, may be short-lived if built on shaky foundations, especially in a VUCA context where myriad risks could derail and even destroy organisations.

Leaders must pay attention to what may go under the radar but is nonetheless critical to an organisation's survival and long-term success. These include daily acts of care, performed by staff at all levels, that forestall human, financial or reputational losses, whether from training accidents, terrorist attacks, data loss or disease outbreaks. Just as critical is the identification of structural weaknesses, vulnerabilities or long-term risks.

Yet what is typically rewarded at the workplace is solving problems that have spilled into the open, rather than timely action that prevents crises from emerging in the first place. When crisis erupts, heads may roll, but fear alone may not be enough to avert preventable failures. Internal audits and risk management protocols have a part to play, but this is also a question of leadership — in particular, the tone which leaders set for the organisation.

Leaders need to make clear that they value the daily exercise of care — such as by walking the ground to observe these efforts, and encouraging and exhorting members of the team. The intent is not to avoid taking calculated risks, but rather to spot vulnerabilities and anticipate threats.

It is also incumbent on leaders to invest in the future — in people and processes, sustainability and resilience. The returns on such investments may not be immediately apparent in financial statements or even during one's tenure in office — but will have a bearing on the organisation's long-term viability and success.

As to who is best placed to skipper the storm-tossed ship, I would go with a person of integrity who consults widely, anticipates hazards and ensures that the ship is in good condition — giving those aboard the conviction they are on the right course, and the confidence to deal with contingencies along the way.

Realism, Rules and Empathy All Matter in a Turbulent World

First published in The Straits Times on 6 April 2022

The war between Russia and Ukraine has drawn a range of responses from governments and citizens around the world. Many have expressed outrage at Russia for its flagrant violation of international law and the growing humanitarian fallout from the invasion. Conversely, among those inclined towards a "realist" interpretation of global affairs, some pin blame for the war on the expansion of NATO to Russia's doorstep.

Realpolitik is a given in an inherently anarchic world; it would be naïve to assume that states are guided by anything beyond self-interest. However, it is in the enlightened self-interest of all nations to uphold and reinforce international law and humanitarian principles as the foundation for a more stable and harmonious world order.

It was not long ago that globalisation seemed inexorable, and with it, a more interdependent, prosperous and peaceful world. Commentators pointed to the rise in multilateral engagement and free trade, the global decline in absolute poverty, as well as the fall in combat deaths from military conflicts over the decades.

QUESTIONING THE PREMISES FOR PEACE

Proponents of "capitalist peace" theory have suggested that growing trade interdependence would reduce the likelihood of armed conflict by tilting nations' cost-benefit appraisals in favour of peace. Other political analysts have claimed evidence of a "democratic peace". This is the hypothesis that democracies are less likely to initiate war, particularly against other democracies, due to greater public accountability, checks and balances. Whereas an absolute ruler may be driven to war by pride or ambition, a democratic government can only garner the requisite public support for war when enough citizens perceive the benefits to outweigh the costs.

There is also the notion that nuclear deterrence has made the world fundamentally safer. By guaranteeing mutually assured destruction, it is believed that no rational state would risk all-out nuclear war. This is of course premised on rationality on the part of decision-makers. Where governments are accountable to the public and decision-making is collective, the likelihood of nuclear warfare appears remote.

In the light of recent developments, however, none of these premises for peace seems particularly compelling. While economic sanctions would not be expected to have much impact on a country as isolated as North Korea, the threat of unprecedented sanctions by the West failed to dissuade Russia from invading Ukraine — this despite Russia being a G20 economy plugged into global networks of trade and investment.

As for democratic peace, humanity's march towards "the end of history" — the "universalisation of Western liberal democracy" according to political scientist Francis Fukuyama — appears to have stalled. In 2021, the Economist Intelligence Unit Democracy Index fell to its lowest level since its inception in 2006, as authoritarianism continued to advance globally.

Republics may themselves be hijacked by demagogues and turned into dictatorships: historical antecedents include the Roman empire and Nazi Germany. Besides the obvious examples of democratic reversals in countries such as Russia, even mature democracies such as the United States could be at risk of sliding into authoritarianism, as American historian Timothy Snyder has warned.

When absolute power is vested in one man or a small coterie of decision-makers, the national good may be subordinated to the aims of self-preservation, ambition or revenge. In such a situation, even nuclear war cannot be ruled out.

SELF-RESTRAINT AND PRUDENCE NEEDED

The fragility of peace impels realism for all actors on the world stage. It calls for self-restraint on the part of major powers, and prudence on the part of small states. Instability is stoked when the world's most powerful states pursue narrow self-interest or overreach on the basis of what they can do rather than what they ought to do. American political scientist John Mearsheimer and other commentators have warned for years that the eastward expansion of NATO would provoke a reaction from the Russian Bear. Russia, too, has now overreached, following its gains from war with Georgia and the annexation of Crimea.

While overreach may ultimately work to the detriment of major powers, their leaders will in all likelihood continue to fall prey to hubris in the pursuit of myopic self-interest. Small nations must therefore recognise the cold logic of great power competition, and make the necessary military and diplomatic preparations on this basis.

This means investing in defence capability and being clear-eyed about geopolitical and security threats. It will not do to put misguided faith in other countries riding to the rescue. There are limits to the help that small states can expect to receive in the event of war. As the Ukraine conflict demonstrates, the United States and European powers are hesitant to risk military confrontation with a nuclear-armed state. Europe's dependence on Russian energy has also circumscribed the political will to step up economic sanctions on Russia.

INTERNATIONAL LAW AND HUMANITARIAN PRINCIPLES MATTER TOO

The acceptance of realpolitik does not imply that governments and citizens should acquiesce to the injustice of war and the contravention of international law. To ignore international law and humanitarian principles would be to accept the law of the jungle, where might is right, and essentially give up on the multilateral project that arose from the ashes of the Second World War.

Given the limitations of the United Nations and the International Court of Justice in their ability to pass resolutions and enforce judgments against errant states, it is the responsibility of all nations to impose costs on states that violate international laws and norms.

Besides, the loss of lives, displacement of millions and injustices suffered should elicit in each of us a human response, regardless of political affiliation or geopolitical leaning. In trying to garner support for Ukraine, it does not help that the West has in the past acted inconsistently with international law and principles, a notable instance being the 2003 US-led invasion of Iraq, which former UN Secretary-General Kofi Annan indicated was not in conformity with the UN charter.

Europeans have also not been as welcoming to refugees of other war-torn nations as they have been with those fleeing Ukraine. This has left the door open to charges of Western hypocrisy and reinforced existing distrust of and antipathy towards the West in many developing countries.

Rather than let Western shortcomings blunt sympathy for Ukraine, surely the correct response should be a greater commitment to uphold international law and ethical principles? While the fallout from the Ukraine war is of a different scale, it is also important to keep the spotlight on the suffering endured by people in other conflict zones, such as Ethiopia, Yemen and Syria. There should not be any forgotten wars, and the international community must be equally seized with the urgency of bringing durable peace to other war-torn nations.

Citizens have a part to play as empathy and moral outrage are not inconsequential in realpolitik. Public opinion has a bearing on foreign and domestic policy in all except the most autocratic states. For instance, citizens of Western nations have to varying extents expressed willingness to accept higher energy costs as a necessary consequence of sanctions on Russia. Multinational corporations, responding to public pressure, have been pulling out of Russia since the onset of the war in Ukraine.

In a world that is in part anarchic and in part rules-based, it is incumbent on governments and citizens to tilt the balance in favour of order and peace. This means condemning violations of international law and norms in unequivocal terms, and seeking to collectively punish infractions as appropriate. A broader view of national interest ought to include the strengthening of the rules-based international order from which most countries, including Singapore, benefit.

Strengthening the Middle Ground

First published in The Straits Times on 3 May 2022, and republished in Berita Harian on 8 May 2022

At the press conference announcing his selection as leader of the People's Action Party fourth generation team, Finance Minister Lawrence Wong alluded to the challenges of greater political contestation and the growing desire for diversity in Parliament.

Questions are already swirling about how politics and governance will evolve as the leadership transition unfolds. In particular, will Singapore continue down the path of increasing political participation and social inclusivity? And how will this evolution affect Singapore's efficiency and distinctiveness?

CITIZENS' EXPECTATIONS

With an increasingly heterogeneous population and greater diversity of views, public consultation will take on even greater importance ahead of major policy decisions. Citizens expect to have their views heard and to participate in the decision-making process. It will not suffice for the Government to involve stakeholders only in implementation — upstream deliberation, too, will no longer be the sole province of policy wonks.

For instance, the Ministry of National Development's public consultation in 2021 yielded many ideas to address the issue of windfall gains from the sale of prime-location flats, while also clarifying the tradeoffs inherent in each of the suggestions. The recently launched White Paper on Singapore Women's Development was the product of a year-long consultation process that engaged nearly 6,000 participants in over 160 conversations.

A more in-depth process of policy deliberation and public consultation can seem time-consuming and inefficient. But the process can uncover policy blindspots, generate fresh ideas for consideration and refine policies before rollout. It also helps to engender the buy-in so crucial for successful policy implementation.

IMPORTANCE OF THE MIDDLE GROUND

Forging a consensus is much easier if there is a strong middle ground of citizens who are well-informed and committed to the national interest. Mutual trust among citizens and stakeholders allows for difficult conversations to take place without exacerbating divisions. It is the mark of a mature society that disagreements can be articulated respectfully without denigrating those who hold a different view.

Laws and policies should reflect the tenor of society in line with majority values, without imposing a "tyranny of the majority". There should be space for responsible public discourse and self-expression — whether on inequality, racism, LGBTQ+, the death penalty or foreign manpower — while avoiding crippling protests or unbridled free speech that can inflame tensions between different groups in society. Stakeholders, including community and religious organisations and civil society groups, can help by exercising their influence responsibly and pursuing their interests in a spirit of give and take.

As Mr Wong pointed out at a forum on tribalism and identity politics last November, the Government can play the role of a fair and honest broker on issues that divide public opinion. This requires a Government that is trusted, responsive and prepared to exercise leadership.

It is heartening that longstanding policies are being reviewed and updated as societal norms evolve. The decision to permit female Muslim nurses to wear a headscarf while in uniform was taken after a process of consultation to make sure that both the Muslim and non-Muslim communities were comfortable with this move.

On other issues, consensus may be difficult to achieve, but it may still be possible to find a workable path forward. The Government is now consulting with diverse groups of Singaporeans to better understand their viewpoints on Section 377A of the Penal Code, which criminalises sex between men.

FOUR WAYS TO BOOST THE CENTRE

It is perhaps a reflection of Singapore's strong middle ground that the ruling party and main opposition party are seen as fairly centrist in their public policy positions. However, this cannot be taken for granted as democratic contestation intensifies. The experience of other countries shows how easy it is to slide into demagoguery, where politicians prey on tribal fears and pit one group against another to advance their electoral prospects. In some instances, this could take the form of divisive communal politics; in others, right-wing populism that veers into xenophobia.

The best antidote is to continually nurture the middle ground in several ways.

First, it is important to pursue both outcome and process legitimacy as the bedrock of effective governance. Singapore's leadership must continue striving to better the lives of citizens through inclusive economic growth, while upholding fairness, transparency and rule of law. Both successful outcomes and fair processes are necessary for broad-based support for the government's agenda, so that extreme views and ideologies are less likely to gain a foothold in politics.

Second, policies that promote social inclusion and reduce socioeconomic disparity will help to prevent the emergence of marginalised communities and groups. There is a need for economic security and social mobility to give citizens a stake in the nation, so that all can aspire to lead a fulfilling life even in a competitive, meritocratic society. Social investment to expand opportunities for Singaporeans from early childhood through to the working years and beyond is vital. So, too, are measures to raise the wages of the lower-income, enhance fiscal progressivity and strengthen social security. Otherwise, issues such as foreign manpower and climate sustainability will more easily divide opinion between the affluent who are well insulated from financial pressures, and those who feel the economic impact of policies much more acutely.

Third, the Government should update policies at a pace that is comfortable for society, in step with evolving norms and values. This is particularly pertinent to issues of conscience and individual rights, where the assertion of such rights may run against traditional societal values. Interest groups are less likely to overreach if they know their views are factored into the decision-making process fairly. Over time, this can nourish a middle ground that is patient and open-minded, in turn expanding the space for societal consensus.

Finally, access to timely and reliable information is a necessary foundation for balanced public discourse. Transparency engenders trust and is vital for Singapore's competitiveness as a global city in the information age. It is better to build up trusted sources of information such as an independent, responsible media rather than to rely on propaganda or censorship.

At the same time, falsehoods must be called out and debunked. This is particularly challenging given the rise in foreign influence campaigns and social media echo chambers. Encouraging responsible and respectful debate can help to improve public understanding and strengthen policymaking.

A strong middle ground may serve as ballast, keeping the polity centred amid the geopolitical tempests that will invariably come our way. In seeking both outcome and process legitimacy, and avoiding the extremes of tribal politics and illiberal conformity, Singapore can aspire to be a "Goldilocks" polity — one that is neither too hot nor too cold, but inclusive and cohesive.

Seizing the Opportunity to Move Singapore Forward

First published in The Straits Times on 5 July 2022

Last week, Deputy Prime Minister Lawrence Wong launched Forward Singapore (Forward SG), a year-long national conversation which aims to harness the views of Singaporeans to shape the nation's future and renew its social compact.

Like previous national conversations, Forward SG is intended to foster trust and collaboration between the political leaders — in this case DPM Wong and his 4th Generation leadership team — and the citizenry. Coming after Our Singapore Conversation (OSC) and the Singapore Together Emerging Stronger Conversations, which covered familiar ground including national identity, opportunities and social support, it may be tempting to dismiss Forward SG as just more of the same.

However, I would argue that Forward SG, if done well, can create significant value through both process and content. This requires stakeholders to approach it with an open mind and a constructive spirit. A few bold process innovations could also set Forward SG apart and generate greater impact.

THERE IS VALUE IN PROCESS

Some may be sceptical that such an exercise can yield major policy breakthroughs, either because most issues have already been discussed exhaustively, or because existing policy paradigms are simply too entrenched to be reshaped. While unrealistic expectations could set up Forward SG for failure, low expectations and ambition will not help either. Regardless of the novelty of ideas that emerge, national conversations like Forward SG recognise the intrinsic value of gathering Singaporeans from all walks of life to talk about issues that matter to them.

Charting Singapore's future is a collective endeavour: it is important for citizens to have a sense of shared ownership of this process. Authentic conversations are therefore crucial. Participants must feel that their views are being heard — that their perspectives matter and that they are not just there to make up the numbers. It is also useful for participants to hear, first-hand, the views of fellow citizens which may be different from their own. As conversations among citizens, and not just between citizens and the state, they can broaden perspectives and promote mutual understanding among societal stakeholders.

It is best not to pre-judge the output of these conversations. Policymakers should keep an open mind, fully prepared to revisit assumptions as they take in the views of different segments of the population. Likewise, citizens should be prepared to have their views and assumptions challenged by fellow participants.

As is often said, no one has a monopoly of wisdom in today's complex world. Approaching Forward SG with a spirit of openness and good faith will enable all to get the most out of the exercise.

NATIONAL UNITY AND RENEWAL

The themes to be covered under Forward SG have been organised into six pillars. These topics may be evergreen, but this is because they are vital for national unity and renewal, on which Singapore's continued success depends. The focus on how to build a Singapore that "benefits many, not a few" — in the words of DPM Wong — is particularly pertinent, given the driving forces, like technological change and global competition, that tend to accentuate inequality and increase precarity among vulnerable groups.

Conversations on shared values bear repeating, as Singapore itself is evolving in terms of the composition of the polity, the life experiences of citizens, as well as the influences and ideologies permeating society. This also makes it critical to re-evaluate and refresh Singapore's concept of meritocracy and the mutual obligations among citizens and the state, which are prerequisites for social cohesion and national unity.

Renewal must extend beyond the social compact to include Singapore's economic model as well. Changing technology and business models, along with reconfiguration of trade flows and supply chains, mean that the existing economic blueprint is no guarantee of future success. It is therefore appropriate that the economy and jobs, along with education and lifelong learning, are among the pillars of Forward SG. Economic strategy is closely intertwined with citizens' aspirations and efforts, and cannot be left to economic committees and the business sector alone.

Singapore may have come far since independence, but it is important not to lose the pioneering spirit that has propelled the country from Third World to First. For similar reasons, Amazon, a highly successful firm, exhorts employees to adopt a "Day 1" mentality: to treat every day like it is the first day in a new start-up. This entails a willingness to test new ideas and try out new ways of doing things.

For a country like Singapore, it is also about openness to talent from abroad. Immigration can revitalise cities with fresh ideas and energy, but could also be disconcerting for locals who may fear competition for jobs and opportunities. Hence, an important part of the national conversation should be on how Singapore can benefit most from openness and immigration, while helping Singaporeans to feel secure and valued in their homeland.

DEEPENING THE CONVERSATION

I expect Forward SG, like previous national conversations, to encompass a range of discussion settings and interfaces — both in-person and online, to draw out different groups of Singaporeans and reach as many as possible.

Taking some risks could set Forward SG apart from previous conversations. For instance, without compromising privacy, conversation transcripts could be released, beyond carefully curated summaries or extracts.

Different ways of presenting synthesised data, such as mindmaps, word clouds or straw poll results, could also give the public a richer flavour of the discussions.

The reflections that emerged from past national conversations have informed policymaking. For instance, Prime Minister Lee Hsien Loong acknowledged the input of OSC at the 2013 National Day Rally, where policy moves to provide greater assurance to Singaporeans in areas such as housing and healthcare were announced. Likewise, the Emerging Stronger Conversations identified concerns and priorities that resonated with Singaporeans, such as mental wellness and sustainability, while providing opportunities to turn ideas into action.

To take the conversations under Forward SG a step further, one possibility is to have participants form working groups to flesh out policy options. Others could then join in the debate, challenging these policy proposals, refining them further or suggesting alternatives. This will enable interested participants to think deeper about issues and consider the tradeoffs inherent in national policies.

Where possible, the Government could provide data to facilitate the deliberations of these groups. Participants would not, of course, have access to the full set of government data, which includes firm-level and individual data, for reasons of confidentiality and national security. Nonetheless, the policy options developed through the engagements could be a valuable resource for the Government. This would require public agencies to be confident, both in the rigour of their policy thinking, as well as in the maturity of citizens, to engage in policy co-creation.

The test-bedding of ground-up solutions, pioneered by the Alliances for Action under Singapore Together, should also continue under Forward SG. This will deepen the partnerships among the public, private and people sectors in bringing about positive change in Singapore.

Forward SG promises to build on the ideas and aspirations expressed by citizens in previous conversations, and will certainly leverage past experience for best practices in citizen engagement. It is my hope that it will also break new ground, both in process and content, to take Singapore forward.

Renewing an Exceptional Singapore

First published in The Straits Times on 27 July 2022

In just under two weeks, Singapore will celebrate its 57th National Day. There is much Singaporeans have to be thankful for as we emerge from the COVID-19 pandemic and reflect on how far the nation has come since independence.

Singapore's journey to this point has been indubitably exceptional — some have called it nothing less than a miracle. The question is: can Singapore scale greater heights in the next 57 years, or will the nation invariably slide into middle-aged, developed country malaise?

This will depend, I believe, on whether Singapore can maintain an edge in areas where it has traditionally excelled, and succeed in building new systemic advantages embedded in people and society. It is worthwhile to first take stock of the national narrative that underpins discussions of what Singapore must do to survive and to thrive. The narrative of competitiveness and vulnerability remains relevant for our time but may be in need of a revamp.

REFURBISHING THE NATIONAL NARRATIVE

Generations of schoolchildren have been told the story of Singapore's unlikely rise — a tiny island state with no natural resources, which through the grit and determination of its people, under farsighted leadership, overcame numerous obstacles and built a nation. In the 1980s and

133

90s, there was a national obsession with being number one — Singapore had the best airport, best airline, busiest sea port, and even the tallest man-made waterfall in Jurong Bird Park. Later, top rankings in global competitiveness indices were celebrated, as were public universities' global rankings and Singapore students' performance in international literacy and numeracy tests.

The desire to be ahead of the competition was accompanied by a profound sense of vulnerability as a small, young nation. Singaporeans have often been reminded of how fragile our society is — hence the need to guard against racial and religious discord, to safeguard national reserves and build a strong armed forces as deterrence against external threats.

Now that Singapore has reached the income levels of advanced economies, and we are able to "punch above our weight" in international influence, some wonder whether the vulnerability narrative is holding us back — whether it ought to be replaced with a more confident posture. Others contend that Singaporeans would do well not to lose sight of our vulnerabilities, given heightened geopolitical contestation and the growing threat of foreign interference and disinformation.

The notion of competitiveness may seem somewhat crass in an age where inclusivity and solidarity are increasingly emphasised. But economic survival and success should not be taken for granted; otherwise, complacency and listlessness can easily set in. What is important to register is that competition is not zero-sum either among citizens or among nations. Competitiveness is in essence about drive and passion — continually pushing the limits of what is possible, to achieve our potential as individuals and as a nation. This could entail collaborating with others for mutual advancement. It follows that competition is not limited to finishing ahead of others, but also about transcending limitations and reaching new heights.

As for Singapore's vulnerabilities, the question should be how to turn these into strengths. It is not about being fatalistic or adopting a defensive mindset, but making a virtue of necessity. Singapore has done this many times before: for instance, addressing water scarcity has transformed Singapore into a hub for cutting-edge water technologies. Our land constraints have led to the development of innovative urban solutions, including high-rise greenery. So even if Singapore is renewable energy-constrained, this should not stymie ambitions to become a clean energy and green technology hub.

The narrative of vulnerability can be paired with one of opportunity and innovation, marrying confidence and circumspection as we address the challenges of the 21st century.

FINANCIAL STRENGTH AND FUTURE-READY INFRASTRUCTURE

The financial reserves which earlier generations have accumulated confer on Singapore a significant advantage today. Besides providing insurance against the proverbial rainy day, the Singapore's past reserves generate investment returns that directly contribute about a fifth of the Government's annual budget. By contrast, many other developed and developing countries rely significantly on borrowing to meet their public spending needs. The reserves will become even more of an asset as interest rates and borrowing costs rise across the world. Stewarding the reserves well will ensure that future generations will continue to enjoy the fruits of this inheritance.

Integral to Singapore's economic success to date has been the development of world-class infrastructure, including our transport and digital hardware. This has enhanced Singapore's connectivity to the world and consolidated our hub status, from which our businesses and workers derive an economic premium. Renewing our infrastructure for the future requires long-term planning and considerable investment. The development of Changi Airport Terminal 5 and 5G infrastructure, for instance, are vital for future economic capacity and growth.

PASSIONATE PEOPLE AND EXCEPTIONAL LEADERS

People have always been seen as Singapore's most important resource. A disciplined and skilled workforce played a key role in Singapore's industrialisation following Independence. Going forward, diligence and competence remain vital workforce traits but are not enough to propel Singapore to the next phase of development. With wages rising to the levels of advanced economies, capabilities will have to increase further if Singapore is to remain competitive. This calls for a spirit of innovation and enterprise in each worker and citizen.

Already, efforts are underway in our schools and tertiary institutions to encourage creativity, risk-taking and innovation. With greater financial resources, more young Singaporeans are pursuing their passion in the arts, sports, hobbies and social causes — some succeeding in turning these into vocations. These pursuits may seem frivolous at first glance, but they augur well for a more innovative Singapore.

It is not just the young who need to be passionate and inventive; in Singapore's greying workforce, Singaporeans of all ages will need to find the spark that turns a job into a calling. If more Singaporeans can find passion and purpose in their work, productivity will increase along with work and overall life satisfaction. This will unlock individual and collective potential, and take the country to the next level.

Exceptional political leadership will continue to be critical for Singapore's success, but the type of leadership needed today may be different from that in the early years of nation-building.

A major difference is that the gap in education and experience between the leadership and the populace has narrowed considerably over the years. Among today's citizens are many well-informed and professionally accomplished people who are inclined to question the government's policies and programmes. A good number may have expertise and experience in business and specific domains beyond what the political leaders possess. Founding Prime Minister Lee Kuan Yew and his comrades walked the ground and consulted widely, but they not did think it necessary to have a "national conversation". Today, citizens expect to be consulted and engaged; indeed, the Government would do well to tap their ideas, energy and resources.

A leader today does not have to be the smartest person available, but he or she must be able to harness the collective wisdom of team members, to provide direction and coordination and to persuade others to get behind a vision. Given the many competing ideologies and interests in today's heterogeneous society, we will still need exceptional leaders, albeit with different strengths from those of yesteryear, to hold the polity together and take the nation forward.

AN EXCEPTIONAL SOCIETY

Countries larger than Singapore have no lack of capable men and women among the ranks of their citizens and leaders. However, many of these states still struggle to pass their legislative agenda, and are beset by infighting, both within and between political parties and their supporters. As a result, considerable time and resources are expended unproductively while society becomes polarised.

For Singapore to continue to thrive, we will need an exceptional society — one that can accommodate different views while fostering a broad unity of purpose and national solidarity. I have written previously about the importance of having a strong middle ground of well-informed, responsible citizens who are committed to the national interest. This will allow the competition of ideas within a democracy to build up rather than tear down society. The evolution of the polity — a task that falls to both citizens and leaders — will perhaps above all else define Singapore's trajectory over the next 57 years.

Home, Truly

First published by TODAY on 8 August 2022 with the title "National Day Special: Why it's getting harder to make Singapore a home truly for all, and yet we must persevere"

Come National Day, we can expect to hear moving renditions of singer-songwriter Dick Lee's composition *Home*. This much-loved National Day song reminds us that home is more than a mere abode — it is a place of familiarity that imbues in us a sense of belonging.

When we speak of Singapore as our home, we may think of both places and people, physical landmarks along with intangible culture. Familiar sights, sounds, tastes and smells all make up our experience of home.

MANY FACETS OF HOME

Most people, unsurprisingly, consider their home country to be their country of citizenship. However, the notion of home transcends legal status and the colour of one's passport: it is also about one's identification with a country and people. This in turn stems from the many facets of home that tug at our heartstrings.

Those who have grown up in Singapore may share a common set of experiences shaped by public housing, the school system and for men, National Service. Integral to our experience of home are memories — of family excursions to familiar locales, hanging out with friends, a first date.

But Singapore is becoming more diverse. Among our population are new citizens who may see Singapore through fresh lenses, whose practices and preferences are informed by their cultural heritage and life experiences elsewhere. They may be in the process of making Singapore their home — forging new ties to people and places as they sink roots here.

While not all Singaporeans will recollect the Singapore of yesteryear, we are building a shared future together. So it is vital for new citizens and old to get to know one another, and for Singaporeans of different races, ages and origins to embrace the rich and evolving cultural tapestry that makes up modern Singapore.

NOTION OF HOME BEING RESHAPED

For many of us, the COVID-19 pandemic has heightened our awareness of home and its significance in our lives. As travel barriers sprung up across the globe in 2020, the world suddenly didn't seem as borderless as before. Citizens who had lived and worked abroad for many years came home to be near loved ones or to avail themselves of vaccines and medical care here.

Over the past two and a half years, Singaporeans who would normally have been travelling overseas became reacquainted with Singapore — exploring what our island has to offer through staycations, nature walks or culinary expeditions.

A 2021 study by Turkish psychologists Meral Gezici Yalçın and N. Ekrem Düzen found that for many, the meaning of home has been reconstructed by the experience of the pandemic. While national lockdowns have imparted negative connotations such as coercion and restrictions, home has also taken on added significance as a safe haven and all-embracing living space.

At the same time, the notion of home is being reinterpreted through the simultaneous rise of nationalism and identity politics in many parts of the world. Right-wing groups in the United States, Europe and Asia are stirring up anti-foreigner sentiment, while various communities are demanding greater rights for members of their tribe or in-group. Societies are fracturing along the lines of race, religion, sexual orientation, ideology and political affiliation, to name a few.

HOME UNDER PRESSURE

Singapore is not immune to these pressures. In fact, our society is becoming more heterogeneous. A range of identity markers — including but no longer limited to race and religion — is distinguishing us as individuals and groups. Nationality, then, becomes just one of the myriad markers of who we are as persons.

Some countries have responded to these challenges by foisting a strong national identity on all citizens, new and old — forcing conformity in ideology, language and dressing, or suppressing competing claims on personal allegiance. Singapore, by contrast, has always allowed its constituent races to retain and express their cultural distinctiveness.

This broad tent mindset should be extended to immigrants and new citizens, as is fitting for a global city and cosmopolitan society. But those who take up citizenships must make the effort to acquaint themselves with local customs and culture. There is no compulsion to shed one's culture of origin, but to embrace the Singapore identity and all that this country has to offer.

With heightened great power contestation, the pull of ethnic and cultural forces beyond our borders may generate strains within our multiethnic society. Various social and political ideologies are also spreading rapidly across borders through social media. Whether Singapore can hold together as a nation depends on whether Singaporeans can learn to live with others who are different, or whether our loyalties are so divided by competing identities that we cannot move forward cohesively as a nation.

AN INCLUSIVE HOME FOR ALL

Looking around the world today, the impact of political and societal fissures is sadly evident. A recent Gallup poll found that Americans' confidence in the Supreme Court has sunk to a historic low amid a heated debate over abortion rights; in England, supporters of a football club regularly boo the national anthem to express their grievances against the state. These offer cautionary tales of what might happen here if groups feel disenfranchised or ignored.

Inclusive policies that affirm all citizens and their place in the nation are therefore important. Public policy has a role to play in setting the tone for the nation, but it too has to reflect the tenor of society — the prevailing social mores and attitudes. Hence both the political leadership and citizenry are responsible for co-creating an inclusive home for all.

Regarding foreign relations or laws on issues such as homosexuality and the death penalty, the Government will invariably take positions that are welcome by some but opposed by others. These are emotive issues for many Singaporeans: our ethnic, religious and other identities may well be bound up in them. The question is whether we debate these issues respectfully, with an open mind and big hearts, and find it in ourselves to stand by our home and fellow citizens even when state policy goes against our personal views and values.

A home is for family, but it should also be welcoming of guests. These include our migrant workers — among them professionals, construction and factory workers, domestic helpers and other service staff. They play vital roles in supporting our economy and society.

Some may interact frequently with locals while others — by choice or necessity — socialise mainly among their compatriots or fellow migrant workers. How we treat the most vulnerable among them is a reflection of our society's values. As hosts, it is incumbent on Singaporeans to make others feel at home in the city we call home.

All said, a home is one that accepts and empowers us. A home makes us secure and confident as individuals, providing the platform from which to spread our wings and take flight, enabling us to sing with all our heart:

This is home, truly
Where I know I must be
Where my dreams wait for me...

Happy National Day.